The LADY *in the* VAN

THE COMPLETE EDITION

by the same author

PLAYS ONE
(*Forty Years On, Getting On, Habeas Corpus, Enjoy*)

PLAYS TWO
(*Kafka's Dick, The Insurance Man, The Old Country,
An Englishman Abroad, A Question of Attribution*)

THE LADY IN THE VAN

OFFICE SUITE

THE MADNESS OF GEORGE III

THE WIND IN THE WILLOWS

THE HISTORY BOYS

THE HABIT OF ART

PEOPLE

HYMN AND COCKTAIL STICKS

television plays

ME, I'M AFRAID OF VIRGINIA WOOLF
(*A Day Out, Sunset Across the Bay, A Visit from Miss Prothero,
Me, I'm Afraid of Virginia Woolf, Green Forms, The Old Crowd, Afternoon Off*)

ROLLING HOME
(*One Fine Day, All Day on the Sands, Our Winnie,
Rolling Home, Marks, Say Something Happened, Intensive Care*)

TALKING HEADS

screenplays

A PRIVATE FUNCTION
(*The Old Crowd, A Private Function, Prick Up Your Ears,
102 Boulevard Haussmann, The Madness of King George*)

THE HISTORY BOYS: THE FILM

autobiography

THE LADY IN THE VAN

WRITING HOME

UNTOLD STORIES

A LIFE LIKE OTHER PEOPLE'S

fiction

THREE STORIES
(*The Laying on of Hands, The Clothes They Stood Up In,
Father! Father! Burning Bright*)

THE UNCOMMON READER

SMUT: TWO UNSEEMLY STORIES

The LADY in the VAN

THE COMPLETE EDITION

Alan Bennett

Adapted from the original stage play
by Alan Bennett

With sketches by David Gentleman

P ff

First published in 2015
by Faber & Faber Limited
74–77 Great Russell Street
London WC1B 3DA
AND
Profile Books
3 Holford Yard, Bevin Way
London WC1X 9HD
www.profilebooks.com

The Lady in the Van was first published in 1989 by London Review of Books
The Lady in the Van is included in Writing Home published by Faber & Faber
and is published as a single edition by Faber & Faber and Profile Books

Typeset by Faber & Faber Ltd
Screenplay typeset by Country Setting, Kingsdown, Kent CT14 8ES
Printed and bound by CPI Group (UK) Ltd, Croydon, CR0 4YY

A CIP record for this book
is available from the British Library

ISBN 978-0-571-32620-4

2 4 6 8 10 9 7 5 3 1

CONTENTS

Foreword by Nicholas Hytner 1

Introduction by Alan Bennett 11

The Lady in the Van, the original memoir by Alan Bennett 49

The Lady in the Van: the Film 91

Cast and Credits 93

The Screenplay 97

FOREWORD

I first went to Alan Bennett's house, where this story happened and where it was filmed, in the autumn of 1989, a few months after Miss Shepherd died. I was there to discuss what would turn out to be the start of a twenty-five-year collaboration that has included seven plays, three movies and so many onstage discussions that my questions and his answers now have the inevitability of a catechism. They almost always include the tale of the lady who drove her van into his front garden and stayed for fifteen years.

I'd seen her around. After I moved to Camden in the early eighties, I used to take the detour round Gloucester Crescent on my way to the High Street, mainly to try to work out which creative titan lived where. The Crescent was home to any number of writers, film and theatre directors, publishers, journalists and artists; and although I discovered that Alan lived at no. 23, I had no idea what the yellow van was about. I wondered whether the derelict old lady who appeared to live in it was his mother, which had I ever got close enough to smell her would have seemed even more far-fetched than it was from a safe distance. I didn't think to ask about her when I finally arrived in the study (nor, it turned out, did most of the people who visited the house when she was in the drive), and I only realised what I'd missed when Alan finally wrote about her in the *London Review of Books*.

He insisted then, and continues to insist, that there was nothing remarkable – and certainly nothing kind – about what strikes everyone else as fifteen years of extreme self-sacrifice. 'She didn't really impinge,' he said at a preliminary readthrough of the screenplay. We were sceptical, but said nothing. As the shoot progressed, and we confronted the daily reality of staging the action, we could – if we needed more room for the camera – move the van out of the way. This was not an option available to the householder when the real van occupied the entire space between his front door and the street. 'She didn't impinge?' said Maggie Smith, every time she had to squeeze past her mobile home. '*Impinge?*'

[2]

She obviously did, and not only on Alan's life. Many of the residents of Gloucester Crescent have been there for decades, and shuddered in horror as our van (there were actually four of them) made its ghostly reappearance. Although there was an element of *Rashômon* about their various versions of her, there was no disagreement about the smell, or about the incongruity of her residence in their oasis of cultured serenity.

I've worked often enough with Alan to share his relish for the kind of single-minded oddball who disrupts the complacent certainties of the English. Mad King George at Windsor, shambolic Hector performing his vaudeville turns for the History Boys in their Sheffield grammar school, W. H. Auden offering blow jobs to visitors to his Oxford rooms, Toad of Toad Hall careering around in fast cars and causing grief to his steadfast riverbank friends (which, in *The Wind in the Willows*, is where Alan and I started) all turn their environments upside down by refusing to play by the rules. Miss Shepherd stands out even in this company, and had the added distinction of challenging the self-satisfactions of her host's own tribe (and mine). She shared with Margaret Thatcher the ability to enrage, to great comic effect, the North London liberals amongst whom she set up home – though it has to be said that many of the residents of Gloucester Crescent were charity itself to their unwashed neighbour, and reserved their contempt for Mrs Thatcher, whose politics were nevertheless some way to the left of Miss Shepherd's.

But if it still seems hard to imagine that you might import Miss Shepherd's particular brand of chaos onto your own front doorstep, the view from the study window helped me understand how Alan survived. I'd sat with him there often enough over the years, but it was only when the van was in situ that I started to get some sense of it as it must have been to the writer who sat at the desk, looking at it. Alan owns up in the film to stealing one of his best lines from Proust. Maybe it goes further than that. As Proust looks out from his apartment in the *hôtel* of the Guermantes, and turns the fashionable comings and goings into art, so Alan looks at the van. And for the part of him that never leaves the study, the activity in and around the van is there not to be suffered, but to be recorded.

The truest thing in what we bill as A Mostly True Story is the sight of Alan Bennett at the desk watching the view of Alan Bennett dealing with the mess spilling out of the van. In early drafts, Bennett the writer popped up all over Camden, a constant source of commentary. Even the final draft sent him, on occasion, into the Crescent to witness his alter ego's latest humiliation.

But as we started to shoot, it became clear that the telling of the story is controlled from the desk. The film emerges from the typewriter; so the writer stays in the study, and only appears in the outside world after Miss Shepherd is dead, when he allows her to take over authorship of her own ending. I hope the movie is as much about how a writer writes, and why he chooses what to write about, as it is about his subject.

It is also about what a writer must do with what happens in front of his nose to turn it into a story worth telling. Always scrupulous about any departure from the historical record (I was the guilty party whenever *The Madness of King George* messed with the facts, which wasn't often), Alan has written into the screenplay not just his gradual and reluctant recognition that his best subject was living on his doorstep, but his struggle to tell her story without occasionally inventing it. His intuitions about her inner life, based on information he discovered after her death, are matched by discoveries about his own: that 'you don't put yourself into what you write – you find yourself there'.

That thought appeared first in Alan's autobiographical play *Cocktail Sticks*, and it was Alex Jennings' performance as Alan Bennett in that play – more authoritative and more revealing than the author's as himself – that brought us back to *The Lady in the Van*, which we'd staged with Maggie Smith as Miss Shepherd in 1999. It was the only one of the shows we've made together that didn't open at the National Theatre (it was produced by Robert Fox in the West End). His subsequent plays became the backbone of the National's repertoire during my twelve years as its director, and virtually every one of the actors in the film was a regular company member during that time – though Maggie herself, to my eternal regret, returned only for a gala celebration of the National's fiftieth birthday.

Maggie was one of the glories of Laurence Olivier's unmatched National Theatre company when it started life at the Old Vic. During its first year, she played in repertoire Desdemona to Olivier's Othello and Myra in Noel Coward's own production of *Hay Fever*, and in the fifty years since, she has continued to command with equal mastery the tragic and comic heights. Miss Shepherd allows her the opportunity to scale both in the same film.

Maggie's presence on a set or in a rehearsal room is exhilarating. She's smarter than everybody else, and sniffs out pretension before it's even come round the corner and said hello. There is nothing she can't do – at more than one point in the film, even stretching her portrayal of Miss Shepherd to include the suggestion that she is simultaneously playing what actually happened and what the writer would have preferred to happen. She is demanding above all of herself, always electrifying when the scene asks most of her. She was hardest on herself during the scene where Miss Shepherd plays the piano in the day centre, despite allowing the camera devastating access to an old woman confronting the end of a life she knows she's thrown away.

This film brings together again three of the team that made *The Madness of King George*, and to whom I owe most of what I know about filmmaking. *King George* was shot on 35 mm film by Andrew Dunn and cut on a Steenbeck editing machine by Tariq Anwar. Twenty years on, they are still my tutors – not least in the possibilities offered by the new digital world, amongst which was the (nearly) effortless splitting in two of Alan Bennett. George Fenton, who arranged Handel for *King George*, here composes a score almost entirely his own, and appears as the conductor of Margaret Fairchild's performance of Chopin's First Piano Concerto. He was the only one of us, apart from Alan himself, who actually knew Miss Shepherd, as he's been familiar with 23 Gloucester Crescent since he was a young actor in Alan's first play. His music is infinitely more vivid than his memory: you don't get much more from him about her than a rueful laugh. The director Stephen Frears, a regular visitor to the Crescent, was more forthcoming. He passed by one day and asked what we were up to. 'Well I won't be paying money to see *that*,' he said firmly, after we'd told him. 'I knew the real thing. You'd be better off making a film about Goebbels.'

To the current residents of Gloucester Crescent I can only offer my thanks. They tolerated the considerable intrusion of a film unit with great good humour, and for several weeks weren't even allowed to park their own cars outside their houses. They permitted us to make a film that shows to a rare degree exactly how it was, where it actually happened. Occasionally, and inevitably, life imitated art. I arrived early one Monday morning to find the art department hurriedly evacuating the van of its contents. It had been left in the drive over the weekend, and a couple of revellers from Camden Town had set up temporary home in it. Miss Shepherd's apparently filthy furnishings were now genuinely filthy. 'Don't tell Maggie! Don't tell Maggie!' they cried as they took the dirty mattresses away to be deep cleaned, then made fake-filthy all over again. So I made up some elaborate story about why we needed to shoot something else before we shot whatever it was that needed her to climb into the van, and I didn't own up to her until six months later.

Alan doesn't live at 23 Gloucester Crescent any more, though when we made the film he still owned it. The emerald and gold plaster walls of the study are not the invention of a production designer: the room is unchanged, precisely as it was when he worked there. It's the room where I talked to him about *The Madness of King George*, *The History Boys* and *The Habit of Art* as well as *The Lady in the Van*, though I was never there for very long, as our working relationship is based less on conversation than on a back and forth of draft after draft, each of them incontinently annotated with my notes and suggestions. These many drafts have ended up in the Bodleian Library in Oxford, to which Alan gifted his entire archive. Future scholars, however, will be less interested in my annotations than in the collected writings of Miss Mary Shepherd. Her pamphlets, her scrawled notes, even her shopping lists were carefully preserved by her landlord and now share the shelves with the First Folio, the Gutenberg Bible and the original conducting score of Handel's *Messiah*. This movie is only one of the consequences of her posthumous fame.

Nicholas Hytner, April 2015

INTRODUCTION

I moved to Gloucester Crescent, Camden Town, in 1969. At £11,500, so then hardly a snip, no. 23 was cheaper than some of the other houses because, imposing and double-fronted though it was and built in 1840, it was smaller than most of the villas in the Crescent and so was unsuitable for the young couples with children who were beginning to colonise this part of North London. Built as superior dwellings for the Victorian middle class, the street coincided with the railways that were then being driven through Camden Town (as in *Dombey and Son*) and, partly as a result, the neighbourhood had gone steadily downhill since, particularly during the Second World War, when many of the villas had been turned into rooming houses. My own house had gas meters in all the upstairs rooms that were a relic of its lodging past and which could still overlap with the present. Early on in my occupancy I opened the door one evening to an old man who was looking for a room there, where he had lodged years ago. At that time I was doing a weekly stint on Ned Sherrin's

TV programme *The Late Show* and the old man (played by John Bird) became the central character in a film in which gentrified neighbours with the relics of a social conscience toured Camden Town (in, absurdly, a Rolls-Royce) trying to find other as yet ungentrified lodgings where he would find a welcome. He ended up in the local Rowton House.

Though in 1969 there were no longer any lodging houses in the Crescent some council properties survived (which they happily still do), except that given the Thatcherite policy of selling off council tenancies, plus the current financial pressures on local authorities, the status of such properties can hardly be secure. It's a form of social cleansing that has been to the detriment of the street, which is these days more homogenous . . . and homogenously rich . . . than it has ever been.

When I moved in the residents were a mixed bag, with among the earliest to put down roots the artist David Gentleman and his wife, who are still there more than fifty years later. There were journalists like the late Nicholas Tomalin and Claire, his biographer wife, novelists like Nicholas Mosley and Alice Thomas Ellis with her publisher husband, Colin Haycraft, together with Jonathan Miller and his wife, Rachel, who had first seen the For Sale sign go up on no. 23 and alerted me. There was an ex-Yugoslav diplomat, a retired naval commander, the widow of Vaughan Williams, the composer, and round the corner in Regent's Park Terrace the novelist Angus Wilson and his partner, Tony Garrett, who were a few doors along from perhaps the most distinguished denizen of all, the writer and critic V. S. Pritchett. Oh and there was also a bishop, the Anglican Bishop of Edmonton.

What had brought them to this corner of London was that it was unsmart, relatively quiet and handy for Regent's Park and the West End. When I was acting in the theatre I could cycle down to Shaftesbury Avenue in twenty minutes and to the BBC in Portland Place even more quickly. The shopping was good, Inverness Street market just round the corner with a dairy, a bakery and a cobbler's all in the same parade and a nearby assortment of Italian and Asian grocers, a wet fish shop, a couple of bookshops and half a dozen second-hand furniture and junk shops. What there was not was Camden Lock, which in the intervening years has swallowed up the indigenous shops and made the area simply a tourist venue.

Included now are excerpts from my diary for 2014 leading up to the making of the film of *The Lady in the Van* that October, with some interpolations from the introduction to the stage play (1999).

6 January 2014

I've learned never entirely to believe in a film until it actually happens but it does seem likely that this autumn we will be shooting *The Lady in the Van*. This is the story of Miss Mary Shepherd, the elderly eccentric who took up residence in my garden in 1974, living there in a van until her death fifteen years later. Maggie Smith played Miss Shepherd on the stage in 1999 and all being well will star in the film with Nicholas Hytner directing. To date I've written two drafts of the script and am halfway through a third.

The house where the story happened is currently lived in by the photographer Antony Crolla though many of my belongings are still in situ. This afternoon I go round to start the lengthy process of clearing out some of the books and papers so that it can be used for filming.

I first saw the house in 1968. It belonged to an American woman who kept parrots and there were perches in the downstairs room and also in its small garden.

I did most of the decorating myself, picking out the blurred and whitewashed frieze in the drawing room with a nail file, a job that these days would be done by steam cleaning, whereas then I was helped by some of the actors in my first play, *Forty Years On*, which was running in the West End. One of the actors was George Fenton, who is doing the music for the film, and another was Keith McNally, the proprietor of Balthazar.

20 February

The walls of the sitting room and the study in Gloucester Crescent are just as I decorated them nearly half a century ago. I have always been quite proud of my efforts, though aware over the years that the finish I achieved has often been thought eccentric.

In 1969, having stripped the walls down to the plaster, I stained the sitting room blue using a polyurethane stain. The plaster was the original lime plaster put on when the house was built in 1840. Lime plaster has many advantages: it's grainy and doesn't soak up the stain like blotting paper as modern plaster tends to do (and which is often brown or pink). All the blemishes of the lime plaster showed through, including the notes to themselves made by the builders and their occasional graffiti. None of this I minded, but blue was not a good colour; it was too cold and for a while I felt I had ruined the room and would have to paper it, which was the last thing I wanted. Then, as an experiment, I tried some yellow stain on a small patch and this turned the wall a vibrant green, too strong I'm sure for many people but for me ideal, so that's how I did the whole room. The study next door I did differently using water-based stains and as the walls here were lime plaster too I painted them in a mixture of umber and orange, yellow and green. This I then washed down and sealed so that the room ended up far better than I could have imagined, taking on the warm shades of the walls of an Italian palazzo (I thought anyway). I am sure a competent scene painter would have been able to achieve the same effects with much less trouble but I'm happy I did it myself. And in the intervening years the colour has not faded and will I trust continue to glow as long as any new owner suffers the original plaster to remain, which is not long probably as there are few houses on the street left in their original trim, today's newcomers seldom moving in until they have ripped the guts out of these decent Victorian villas to turn them into models of white and modish minimalism.

In the colourful and variegated background of Camden Town Miss Mary Shepherd, whose strange story the film tells, seems in some respects not unusual. She was a vagrant but a stationary one, resident for the last fifteen years of her life a few feet from my front door where there was a paved area ... the architect had wishfully called it a patio ... just big enough to take a car. Or, as it transpired, a van.

The neighbourhood has never been without its eccentrics, a steady assortment of which were supplied by Arlington House, one of the Rowton Houses put up in the nineteenth century to provide respectable working men with bed and board at a reasonable rate. And so it admirably did though it also housed some unusual characters, one or two of them straight out of Samuel Beckett. Roaming the streets besides was a cast of itinerant alcoholics who roosted the steps of any empty premises or the vicinity of any warm-air outlet. If Miss Shepherd stood out in this company it was not as she perhaps imagined on account of some degree of social superiority but because she had, however decrepit, a place of her own in the shape of the van. She never had to sleep in a doorway, for instance, as many of the men did who had not managed to be taken in at Arlington House.

If, at the foot of the slope of Gloucester Crescent, Arlington House was a secular refuge for the poor and homeless, its spiritual counterpart was the convent opposite the top of the street. This unlovely building, now North Bridge House School, was then still a convent which, though I did not know it, had briefly housed Miss Shepherd herself. For much of the time I lived in the Crescent there was a crucifix on its pebble-dashed wall that overlooked the traffic lights of Gloucester Gate and Parkway. Some time in the 1980s the convent was transmuted into a Japanese school, in the process, understandably perhaps, losing the crucifix. Then it became a private school. Though no fan of private education what made me cross was the selfish parking habits of the parents, particularly when retrieving their children. As they park, I used to think, so do they educate.

My decision to invite Miss S. to put the van in my drive in 1974 was taken reluctantly but the construction put upon it in the film seems to me true to the facts. In the street the van was parked directly opposite the table in the bay window where I did my work. Anything that happened to Miss Shepherd . . . from the everyday skirmishes she had with neighbours and passers-by to the more serious provocations regularly visited on her by hooligans or the malevolent . . . all these were a distraction to me when I was trying to write. Moving Miss S. into the garden got her out of the way of passers-by and the curious so that both of us could thereby have a quieter life and I could for much of the time forget about her – much, as AB points out, like a marriage.

But it was this element of self-interest or self-concern about the move which has always made me reluctant to consider it an act of charity. I was looking after myself, Miss Shepherd only incidentally; kindness didn't really come into it.

The idea that marrying is sometimes the way men choose to forget someone is a (rather crude) Proustian notion, with Swann wedding Odette in order to do just that. And there are a cluster of related aphorisms.

'Good nature, or what is often considered as such, is the most selfish of all the virtues: it is nine times out of ten mere indolence of disposition.'

This is a quotation from William Hazlitt's 'On the Knowledge of Character' (1822) but I didn't find it from reading Hazlitt, whom I've never managed to get into, but quoted in John Osborne's autobiography, *Almost a Gentleman*.

A similar note is struck by George Eliot in *Romola* (1862–3): 'The elements of kindness and self-indulgence are hard to distinguish in a soft nature', which is another quotation I did not find at source but quoted in the *Notebooks* of Geoffrey Madan.

'No man deserves to be praised for his goodness unless he has the strength of character to be wicked. All other goodness is generally nothing but indolence or impotence of will.' (La Rochefoucauld)

The person who never felt the need to go in for such moral analysis and who I'm sure didn't think it was kindness if she ever gave it a thought was, of course, Miss Shepherd herself, parking in my drive a favour she was doing me not the other way round. To have allowed herself to feel in the least bit grateful would have been a chink in her necessary armour, braced as she always was against the world.

'It wasn't a marriage. She wasn't my life,' AB says in one exchange, later cut, though the van always came in handy as a conversation piece. I don't have much small talk so for anyone landed with me at a party, say, 'How's your old lady?' was a good standby. That she had become even in her lifetime something of a celebrity would not have surprised her and she would also consider it entirely fitting that some of her pamphlets are now deposited in the Bodleian Library at Oxford, where Maggie Smith was able to consult them before doing the film.

Miss Shepherd's presence in the garden didn't, of course, stop me jotting things down, making notes on her activities and chronicling her various comic encounters. Indeed, in my bleaker moments it sometimes seemed that this was all there was to note down since nothing else was happening to me.

Still, there was no question of writing or publishing anything about her until she was dead or gone from the garden, and as time passed the two came to seem the same thing. Occasionally newspapers took an interest and tried to blow the situation up into a jolly news item, but the ramparts of privacy were more impregnable in those pre-Murdoch days and she was generally left to herself. Even journalists who came to interview me were often too polite to ask what an (increasingly whiffy) old van was doing parked a few feet from my door. If they did enquire I would explain, while asking them to keep it to themselves, which they invariably did. I can't think that these days there would be similar discretion.

Miss Shepherd helped, lying low if anybody came to my door, and at night straight away switching off her light whenever she heard a footstep. But though she was undoubtedly a recluse, Miss Shepherd was not averse to the occasional bout of celebrity. I came back one day to find her posing beside the van for a woman columnist (gender did count with Miss S.) who had somehow sweet-talked her into giving an interview, Miss Shepherd managing in the process to imply that I had over the years systematically stifled her voice. If she has since achieved any fame or notoriety through my having written about her, I suspect she would think it no more than her due and that her position as writer of pamphlets and political commentator entitled her to public recognition or, as she says in the play, 'the freedom of the land'.

It was imaginary celebrity – I think the psychological term for it is 'delusion of reference' – that made her assume with every IRA bomb that she was next on the list. A disastrous fire in the Isle of Man meant, she was certain, that the culprit would now target her, and had she been alive at the time of Princess Diana's death she would have taken it as a personal warning to avoid travelling (in the van as distinct from a high-powered Mercedes) under the Pont de l'Alma. In the first (and much longer) draft of the play this obsession was examined in more detail:

MISS S.: Mr Bennett. Will you look under the van?

AB: What for?

MISS S.: One of these explosive devices. There was another bomb last night and I think I may be the next on the list.

AB: Why you?

MISS S.: Because of Fidelis Party. The IRA may have got wind of it with a view to thwarting of reconciliation attempts, possibly. Look under the van.

AB: I can't see anything because of all your plastic bags.

MISS S.: Yes and the explosive's plastic so it wouldn't show, possibly. Are there any wires? The wireless tells you to look for wires. Nothing that looks like a timing device?

AB: There's an old biscuit tin.

MISS S.: No. That's not a bomb. It's just something that was on offer at Finefare. I ought to have special protection with being a party leader, increased risk through subverting of democracy, possibly.

AB: Nobody knows that you're a leader of a party.

MISS S.: Well, it was on an anonymous footing but somebody may have spilled the beans. No organisation is watertight.

It's said of Robert Lowell that when he regularly went off his head it took the form of thinking he could rub shoulders with Beethoven, Voltaire and other all-time greats, with whom he considered himself to be on equal terms. (Actually, Isaiah Berlin, about whose sanity there was no doubt, made exactly the same assumption but that's by the way.) The Virgin Mary excepted, Miss Shepherd's sights were set rather lower. Her assumed equals were Harold Wilson, Mr Heath and (as she always called him) 'Enoch', and I was constantly being badgered to find out their private addresses so that they could be sent the latest copy of *True View*. Atypically for someone unbalanced, Miss Shepherd never seemed to take much interest in the Royal Family, the Queen and the Duke of Edinburgh never thought of as potential readers.

Miss Shepherd would be no more happy with the notion of AB as her carer than I was ... and not because 'He's a Communist, possibly'. God apart, she would not presumably have thought herself beholden to anybody ... hence her seeming ingratitude for any form of benevolence; clothes, vans, crème brûlée ... they all involved obligations for which she had no time. The only obligation that counted was the forgiveness of sin ... her sin.

We shared, though, a distrust of caring and perhaps the most heartfelt statement I put into the mouth of AB in the film is his diatribe against caring. He does not like the word; is uncomfortable in the role, which it never occurs to him can be so called until it is suggested by the social worker. The word carries an implication of feeling, a coating of concern not just caring but caring *for*, whereas with me, feeling scarcely entered into it and this may well not be uncommon. Caring, as often as not, is coping with, being landed with, being stuck with, having no choice about. How seldom is it gladly or willingly undertaken? Caring all too often is grudging. Nor is it, as the word implies, a gentle business. 'We have to do everything for her/him means we have to do one thing for them.' Caring is about piss and shit ... shit on AB's shoes when walking past the van, shit on the path when one of the bags Miss S. hurls out hits the ground and bursts. And these are the most minor inconveniences. I never had to haul down her many contoured underthings to wipe her bum, or haul off her sodden knickers ... I never had to unfurl her terrible stockings; still less breach the inner citadel of her castle of clothes ... the routine menialities of real carers, which, we console ourselves, are made tolerable by the love they bear their charges. But one thinks, too, of ageing offspring who are forced into caring for their even more aged parents when all too often they have long since ceased to care for them much or even at all ... or are only caring for them now in grudging recompense for the caring they themselves received long ago.

With me, kindness was never less kindly nor caring so uncaring with exasperation and self-reproach so often the order of the day.

24 September

I open the paper this morning to find that the Dowager Duchess of Devonshire has died . . . or Debo as everybody called her, but not me, as when I first got to know her I felt our acquaintance was too brief for such familiarity and so ended up calling her 'Ms Debo', while I was 'Mr Alan'. The darling of the *Spectator* and a stalwart of the Countryside Alliance, she was hardly up my street, but when she wrote asking if I would write an introduction for one of her books I could not have been more flattered had it been Virginia Woolf wanting a preface to *Mrs Dalloway*. Once the request was made, I knew there was no refusing it and I wrote that the only woman with a will of comparable iron to Debo was Miss Shepherd. Thereafter Debo signed all her letters to me 'D. Shepherd', liking the notion that there might be a seventh Mitford sister, one living in Chatsworth, the other in a broken-down Commer van.

6 October

The first morning of filming for *The Lady in the Van* and I sit in what was once my study, the room now bare and cold, the walls plain plaster, just as it was when I first saw the house in 1968 though I've no memory of being shown it by the estate agent, which is an early shot in the film. Alex Jennings is playing me and looks remarkably like, with no hint of the outrageous blond there sometimes was in *Cocktail Sticks* when he played me on the stage.

The cast of *The History Boys* are in the film for sentimental reasons and because we enjoy working together, even if some have only one line. Today it's Sam Anderson, now a star of *Doctor Who*, who does the opening shot as a Jehovah's Witness:

'Does Jesus Christ dwell in this house?'

Alex Jennings/AB: 'No. Try the van.'

As always on a film I feel a bit lost, the writer not having a proper function and seldom called upon. After weeks of warm sunny weather today is wet and cold and as Maggie Smith goes out for her first shot she says out of the corner of her mouth, 'Thanks a million.'

7 October

Still not settled in and at one point I find myself perched on top of a dustbin behind the front gate until Sam, the nice PA, finds me a proper seat. I was always led to expect that the director and the stars had their names stencilled on the back of their chosen chairs but in forty or so years filming I've never actually seen it, the productions not grand enough maybe. I know the cameraman Andrew Dunn as he filmed *The Madness of King George* and *The History Boys* and though he's always preoccupied I've never seen him out of temper, so that his benevolence and Nick Hytner's cheerfulness infect the unit. It was not always so, with the cameraman often moodier and more temperamental than the actors. When I started there was almost invariably a degree of ill feeling between the sound department and the camera, with sound complaining that the shot as set up made their job impossible. ('Can't get in there, guv.') That's long gone, the only vestige of it being that sound are generally more forthcoming than the camera crew, who are more self-contained and set more store by their expertise.

Roger Allam and Deborah Findlay play the neighbours opposite, outside whose house Miss Shepherd parks. They aren't modelled on the actual neighbours (who had triplets). The only properly named neighbour is Ursula Vaughan Williams, the composer's widow, who is played by Frances de la Tour. Most of the actors have been in stuff of mine before but not Roger Allam, who has been in practically every play Michael Frayn has written. And I can see why as he's subtle and funny and as good off-screen as on.

Taking it all in is David Gentleman. At eighty-odd he stands for all of two hours together sketching what's going on, delighted at having such a subject on his doorstep.

11 October

Come away around 4.30, weary rather than exhausted as I've contributed very little, my only suggestion being that Alex Jennings, who is eating an egg sandwich, should drop some of the egg down his pullover, as I invariably do. The costume department seize on this as a piece of cinéma vérité and egg is accordingly smeared down his front. It hardly seems a day's work.

Having two Alan Bennetts was a feature of the stage production though there they were played by different actors. Having them both played by Alex Jennings is harder to establish, particularly at the outset, but the notion that one part of myself dealt with this awkward demanding woman while another part of myself watched myself doing so, often noting it down, was very much what it felt like when it was happening. 'Living', as Camus said, 'slightly the opposite of expressing.'

There were times, too, when it seemed, grimly affianced as we were, that this was the only thing that was worthy of note, even if Miss Shepherd's presence was so prolonged and taken for granted that the idea I would ever be able to turn it into a book, still less literature, seemed absurd. Also absurd was the notion that she was literary raw material and that this was why I'd invited her in to start with . . . Except of course, if one writes . . . and by the mid 1980s I'd eventually come to the conclusion that this was what I did and that I was indeed 'a writer' . . . then whatever happens is grist to some creative mill, though without any certainty as to its eventual outcome.

15 October

Telling the truth crops up quite a bit in the film, what Miss Shepherd did or didn't do a subject of some disagreement between the two Alan Bennetts. They call not telling the truth 'lying', but 'the imagination' would be a kinder way of putting it, with Alan Bennett the writer finally winning through to make Miss Shepherd talk of her past (as she never actually did) and even to bring her back from the dead in order to take her bodily up to heaven (also imaginary). These departures from the facts were genuinely hard-won and took some coming to, causing me to reflect, not for the first time, that the biggest handicap for a writer is to have had a decent upbringing. Brought up not to lie or show off, I was temperamentally inclined to do both, particularly as a small child, and though reining me in perhaps improved my character it was no help in my future profession, where lying, or romancing anyway, is the essence of it. Nor did my education help. One of the difficulties I had in writing *The Madness of George III* was that, having been educated as a historian, I found it hard ever to take leave of the facts. With George III's first bout of madness the facts needed scarcely any alteration to make them dramatic and only a little tweaking was required but even that I found hard to do.

Never strong on invention I have kept pretty closely to the facts of Miss Shepherd's life, the one exception being the character of the ex-policeman Underwood who figures also in the stage play. He is fictional. That Miss Shepherd had an accident in which a motor cyclist crashed fatally into the van was told me by her brother after her death. It was not her fault but leaving the scene of the accident before the police arrived she was technically guilty of a felony and thus open to blackmail. Underwood is played by Jim Broadbent, with whom I last worked in *The Insurance Man*, a film about Kafka directed by Richard Eyre which we did in Liverpool in 1985, since when Jim has become an international film star much as Pete Postlethwaite did, while seeming no older than he did thirty years back. He's instantly authentic (it's the haircut, I decide), both funny and sinister, and it reminds me how working with him and Julie Walters years ago I used to despair because their casual conversation was funnier and livelier than anything I could dream up. Jim has the ability to look utterly ordinary, certainly in the streets of Camden Town, and though there's no hint of it in the script one would know just from his walk that he's an ex-policeman.

16 October

On one occasion Miss Shepherd claimed to have seen a boa constrictor in Parkway 'and it looked as if it was heading for the van'. At the time I dismissed serpent-sighting as just another of Miss S.'s not infrequent visions . . . boa constrictors, Mr Khrushchev and (putting in regular appearances) the Virgin Mary; the dramatis personae of her visions always rich and varied.

It turned out, however, that on this particular occasion Palmer's, the old-fashioned pet shop in Parkway ('Talking parrots, monkeys, naturalists'), had been broken into, so a boa constrictor on the loose and gliding up the street wasn't entirely out of the question though whether it had a meaningful glint in its eye is more debatable.

This morning we film the sighting of the snake in one of the Gloucester Crescent gardens. And a proper snake it is, too . . . a real boa constrictor, all of nine foot long and answering to the name of Ayesha, which has made the journey from Chipping Norton together with her slightly smaller friend and companion Clementine, both in the care of their handler.

I have had unfortunate experiences with animal handlers as indeed has Maggie Smith, who once had to vault over a stampeding porker during the shooting of *A Private Function*. To be fair, today's handler seems sensible and (unlike the pig handler) unopinionated and since Ayesha doesn't have anything taxing to do in the way of acting, confines himself to making her and Clementine comfortable on a bed of hot-water bottles.

17 October

We're not shooting in sequence so only ten days into the schedule we do the ending of the film. As written ten years or so after Miss S. died (she died in 1989) I'd imagined a blue plaque to her being unveiled on the wall of no. 23. Nick has made this wittier by having the camera pull back to show today's film crew recording the scene watched by various real-life neighbours from the Crescent. This is also their small reward for their being so forbearing about the inevitable inconvenience the film has involved, except, as I wrote to all of them beforehand, though it would involve them being denied their parking rights for six weeks, housing Miss Shepherd had meant I was deprived of my parking rights for fifteen years. In the event, the scene turns out not quite as I'd imagined. There's a blue plaque on the wall, with a crowd of neighbours including Antony Crolla, who lives in the house, and my (slightly embarrassed) partner Rupert Thomas but then the camera (on a crane) catches me higher up the street as I bike down to the set. I get off my bike and join the crowd as Alex Jennings makes a little speech about Miss S., pulls the cord and the camera dollies back to reveal the rest of the crew.

The plaque looks good and genuine, made, I believe out of some rubbery material. I'm hoping it can be left in situ when the film is finished as it may enhance the value of the property thus compensating for the dilapidations consequent on filming and the company getting the house on the cheap.

I have previous form when it comes to unveiling blue plaques as a few years ago I had to pull the cord on the plaque for the peppery painter William Roberts's ex-house in St Mark's Crescent. It's a street that's well supplied with such commemorations. Whereas my own street boasts only one, to Dr Jose Rizal, Writer and National Hero of the Philippines, St Mark's Crescent has at least three, Arthur Hugh Clough, William Roberts and A. J. P. Taylor. There is one to Sylvia Plath where she lived in Chalcot Square but not in Fitzroy Road where she died. The same house, though, has one to Yeats, of whom the late Eric Korn claimed to have heard a passer-by saying, 'Yes, it's a tablet to William Butler Yeast', at which Eric was tempted to add 'who was responsible for the Easter Rising'.

22 October

We are using several vans in varying stages of dilapidation including one smart number in its original trim given to Miss Shepherd some time in the seventies by Lady Wiggin, a Catholic well-wisher from Regent's Park Terrace. Smart as it was, Miss Shepherd still gave it her usual treatment, coating it in lumpy yellow paint (lumpy because she had somehow mixed it with Madeira cake), which she applied with a washing-up brush. Consequent on these vehicular permutations, for the purposes of filming the contents of one van have to be taken out and installed in its successor. I sit in my chair on the pavement watching this wearisome process at work and marvelling at the dedication and conscientiousness of Katie Money and the props department who have it to do. Miss S.'s belongings consist of mountains of old clothes, carrier bags stuffed with her papers interspersed with the contents of her larder, half-eaten tins of baked beans, packets of stale sliced bread, loose onions (which she ate raw), rotting apples and wilting celery and dressed over all with half-used toilet rolls, dirty dusters and soiled Kleenex that one didn't like to look at too closely.

It would be entirely possible to mock up this distasteful agglomeration with some underlying bean bags, plus a top-dressing of eye-catching refuse. The camera wouldn't know. But the actors would. So all this detritus is repeatedly and meticulously transferred from van to van as if it were the contents of an eighteenth-century salon. I know this devotion to duty has nothing to do with me personally but I'm the one who has set it all in motion and I would like to shake all their hands . . . the boy who carefully transfers the opened can of congealed tomato soup, Katie who delicately repositions the dog-eared pack of incontinence pads and puts one of them to dry, as Miss Shepherd did, over the electric ring. I am in all their debt. Instead one of them breaks off to see if she can fetch me a cup of tea.

24 October

Included in the street picture are various passers-by, 'Background action' it's called, as extras walk up or down the street in the back of a scene being played in the foreground. One knows that these characters are actors because they are got up in the fashions of the period and it's particularly noticeable if they're wearing flares or have long hair. The trouble is the street can't be entirely closed off so also coming by are entirely authentic people who are sometimes quite eccentric too and one isn't always sure who are actors and who not. Sometimes, though, it doesn't matter: this morning A. N. Wilson cycles past in his raincoat and beret and he could have been cycling by in 1970.

27 October

Late going round to the unit this morning to find them about to film the scene when manure was being delivered to no. 23, whereupon Miss S. came hurrying over to complain about the stench and to ask me to put a notice up to tell passers-by that the smell was from the manure not her.

Having done one take we are about to go again when it occurs to me that the manure, if fresh, would probably be steaming, as I seem to recall it doing at the time. While this is generally agreed, no one can think of a way of making the (rather straw-orientated) manure we are using steam convincingly. Dry ice won't do it and kettles of hot water prove too laborious. So in the end we go with it unsteaming, the net result of my intervention being that whereas previously everybody was happy with the shot, now thanks to me it doesn't seem quite satisfactory.

28 October

We film a scene in which AB is interviewed about his work by an American journalist, in the course of which he gives her tea and (though I hadn't specified this) cake. Props have opted for Battenberg, which is not a confection I'm much drawn to (I've never liked almond paste), but my tentative enquiry about the availability of Madeira produces howls of merriment and so we go with the Battenberg. It's not that I'm unhappy about this but taken with yesterday's intervention when I brought the production to a halt over the steam from the manure I think I must learn to keep my own counsel.

2 November

Miss S.'s funeral, which in life (or in death) was at Our Lady of Hal in Arlington Road but in the film is at St Silas's at the foot of Haverstock Hill. We also film Miss S. at mass with Maggie Smith at the communion rail. But not just kneeling. After Miss S.'s death I had a letter from Father Cormac Rigby, who was twenty years an announcer on BBC Radio 3 before leaving the Corporation and being ordained a priest in 1985 when he was sent to live at Our Lady of Hal, Miss S.'s local church. He told me how seeing her in the congregation his heart would sink as he had a bad back and Miss S.'s exigent (though not ostentatious) piety required her virtually to prostrate herself when receiving the host, with the priest thus having to follow her right down in order to post the wafer in her mouth. Maggie does this, too, on her knees, four or five times without complaint or assistance. She's a few months younger than me but I couldn't kneel like this or if I went down couldn't get up again. She does both and on camera. Now she goes into the confessional box to unburden herself for the umpteenth time to the long-suffering priest (Dermot Crowley), telling him about the motor cyclist she thinks she killed in an accident years ago. He has heard it all before and has absolved her many times. 'Absolution, my child, is not like the bus pass. It does not run out.' Later when the next in the confessional queue (Clive Merrison) enters the box he staggers back on account of the stench she has left behind her. The priest is unsurprised and we hear his tranquil voice, 'There is air freshener behind the crucifix.'

It was Father Cormac Rigby who told me, as much, I felt, out of kindness as conviction, that my taking in Miss Shepherd would speed my passage through Purgatory. I am not banking on it.

6 November

A wet morning and today we are filming Miss S.'s burial in Kensal Green cemetery. In fact she is buried in an unmarked grave in Camden and Islington cemetery out near the North Circular Road but Kensal Green is more photogenic. It's cold and drizzling with the actors under umbrellas until the moment before 'Action!' when the puddles are briskly swept from the path before the actors stroll down. At one point I see Andrew Dunn delicately remove a noticeable leaf from the path of the camera with all the care of a caddy setting up a putt in golf. Despite the rain Maggie remains good-tempered if subdued though the moment the shot is called she is straightaway full of energy and in good voice. We look at the dignified grave of Alfred Waterhouse, the Victorian architect and painter, and she becomes hysterical over a family plot with a long list of those here interred which ends up, 'Dora is elsewhere'.

The crucial shot of the day (still raining) comes when the dead Miss Shepherd reappears from the grave and discovers the young biker whom she's always thought she'd killed having a fag behind a gravestone. She walks off with him arm in arm into her own personal sunset and as she does so lets out a cackle. 'Mr Bennett. Do you know what that is? It's the last laugh!' Thereafter . . . and by some technical wizardry I don't understand . . . she will ascend into heaven.

12 November

To the National Theatre where Alex J. is filmed on the stage of the Lyttelton, set up for part of the *Talking Heads* monologue 'A Chip in the Sugar'. It was when we were previewing the stage production at Guildford that I dried three times during the same performance, the stage fright that resulted curing me of any desire to act on the stage. It's a year ago now since the National Theatre Fiftieth Anniversary Gala where I played Richard Griffiths' role in an extract from *The History Boys* and the terror has not subsided. Talk I can do and read but act (and, essentially, remember), not any more.

13 November

One of the small pleasures of living in Gloucester Crescent/ NW1 and one which went unmentioned in the (ever more lavish) brochures put out by the (ever more present) estate agents was waking around six in the morning to the sound of distant horses. Still in those days billeted in St John's Wood the King's Troop regularly exercised in Regent's Park, which would occasionally bring them along Oval Road and down the Crescent. The ancient sound of horsemen carried in the early morning air so one would hear the troop long before they cantered into view, twenty or thirty horses, with each khaki-clad soldier leading another riderless mount. The mood of this troop was often quite festive and carefree, in spring a rider plucking down a gout of cherry blossom and putting it in his hat, and in winter there would be some sly snowballing. I always got up to watch them go by and on occasion Miss Shepherd would observe her own stand-to, a young soldier once giving her a mock salute. In summer I fancy they were in shirt-sleeve order, but even when they were more formally dressed it was a relaxed performance, which in winter was made more romantic as the riders materialised out of the gloom, preceded by a lone horseman with a lantern, another outrider with a lamp bringing up the rear. Somewhere in London I imagine this spectacle still goes on but St John's Wood Barracks has gone and it's Camden Town's loss – and since the Guards can't trek over from Hyde Park, the film's loss too.

November, Shoreditch Town Hall

Today we film the young Miss Shepherd as the soloist in a symphony concert in the forties playing Chopin's First Piano Concerto.

I lived briefly in Shoreditch when I first came to London in 1961, lodging with some friends from Oxford in Worship Street, cycling to work during the day at the Public Record Office, then in Chancery Lane, and in the evening at the Fortune Theatre, where I was in the revue *Beyond the Fringe*. The house where we all lived was designed by Philip Webb, the disciple of William Morris, and was something of a social departure, one of a terrace of model dwellings with workshops on the ground floor and accommodation above. Happily it still stands and is now listed. Shoreditch then had little to recommend it, a quarter of small factories and workshops, greasy spoon cafes and furniture menders. Having scarcely been in the neighbourhood since, I am taken aback by how smart and indeed trendy it seems to be, the Victorian tenements and cottages gentrified, the streets lined with modish shops and eateries. The Town Hall, though, has not changed and its elaborately tiled and plastered hall this morning hosts the London Symphony Orchestra, who are being conducted by George Fenton. Wearing his father's tails he has been given a moustache in order to suggest a young Adrian Boult . . . a forlorn attempt as Adrian Boult can never have been young and if George looks like anybody it's Flash Harry, Malcolm Sargent. Happily he's not just acting the conductor, having in his time waved his baton (one of Karajan's batons) at the Berlin Philharmonic and the LA Philharmonic. The young soloist, Clare Hammond, plays well too and filmed in longish takes the music is a pleasure to listen to. Half my life is here, I think as I sit listening, as George was in my first play, *Forty Years On*, and learned his music sitting beside Carl Davis, who played the school organist of Albion House.

I have allowed myself a little leeway in speculating about Miss Shepherd's concert career, except that if, as her brother said, she had studied with Alfred Cortot she must have been a pianist of some ability. Cortot was the leading French pianist between the wars, Miss Shepherd presumably studying with him at the height of his fame. Continuing to give concerts throughout the Occupation, he finished the war under a cloud and it was perhaps this that sent him on a concert tour to England, where I remember seeing his photograph on posters some time in the late forties. Perhaps Miss Shepherd saw it too, though by this time her hopes of a concert career must have been fading, a vocation as a nun already her goal.

Her war had been spent driving ambulances, a job for which she had presumably enlisted and been trained and which marked the beginning of her lifelong fascination with anything on wheels. Comically she figures in my mind alongside the Queen who, as Princess Elizabeth, also did war service and as an ATS recruit was filmed in a famous piece of wartime propaganda changing the wheel on an army lorry, a vehicle my mother fondly believed HRH drove for the duration of hostilities.

What with land girls, nurses, Waafs, the ATS and Wrens, these were years of cheerful, confident, seemingly carefree women and I'd like to think of Miss Shepherd as briefly one of them, having the time of her life: accompanying a singsong in the NAAFI perhaps, snatching a

meal in a British restaurant, then going to the pictures to see Les-
lie Howard or Joan Fontaine. It was maybe this taste of wartime
independence that later unsuited her for the veil or it may be, as
her brother suggested, that she suffered shellshock after a bomb
exploded near her ambulance. At any rate she was invalided out
and this was when her troubles began, with, in her brother's view,
the call of the convent a part of it.

I would have liked her concert career to have outlasted the
war or to have resumed after the duration, when the notion of a
woman playing the piano against the psychological odds was the
theme of the film *The Seventh Veil* (1945) with Ann Todd as the
pianist Francesca and James Mason her tyrannical stick-wielding
Svengali. Enormously popular at the time (and with it the
Grieg Piano Concerto), the film set the tone for a generation of
glamorous pianists, best known of whom was Eileen Joyce, who
was reputed to change her frock between movements.

The Seventh Veil was subsequently adapted for the stage and

I still have the programme of the matinee I saw at
the Grand Theatre in Leeds in March 1951. The
Grieg Concerto had by this time been replaced
by Rachmaninov No. 2 and James Mason by Leo
Genn, but it was still Ann Todd, her guardian as
ever bringing his stick down across her fingers
as she cowered at the keyboard.

If Miss Shepherd had ever made it to the
concert circuit this would be when I might
have seen her, as I was by now going every
week to symphony concerts in Leeds Town

Hall where Miss Shepherd
would have taken her
place alongside Daphne
Spottiswoode or Phyllis
Sellick, Moura Lympany,
Valda Aveling and Gina
Bachauer – artistes with their

décolleté shawl-collared gowns as glamorous and imposing in my
fourteen-year-old eyes as fashion models, Barbara Goalens of the
keyboard, brought to their feet by the conductor to acknowledge
the applause, clutching to their bosoms the bouquets with which
they were invariably presented, to which Miss Shepherd on the
last night of her life contemptuously compares the scrutty bunch
of anemones which AB brings her.

And it was the last night of her life. When I wrote the
original account I glossed over the fact that Miss Shepherd's
death occurred the same night that, washed and in clean things,
she returned from the day centre. I chose not to make this plain
because for Miss Shepherd to die then seemed so handy and
convenient, just when a writer would (if a little obviously) have
chosen for her to die. So I note that I was nervous not only of
altering the facts to suit the drama but of even seeming to have
altered them.

25 November

Today is the last day of shooting and it's as cold and wet as it
was six weeks ago when we started. Today comes the last of the
ex-History Boys, Russell Tovey, who plays a dubious youth, and

whom I at first don't recognise because of his curly black wig. He only has one line, 'Who's the old bat?' but as he passes the van Maggie has to stick her head out and look after him as he goes.

> Miss S.: Mr Bennett. That young man. Did he have an earring?
> AB: He did.
> Miss S.: You want to be careful . . .

Don't go around saying goodbye as at this stage I'm going to the Wrap Party but when Thursday night comes I can't face it.

There is an odd footnote to Miss Shepherd's story that persists into the present day, as resident in Chiswick until her death quite recently was another lady in a van. This might not seem so odd except that she, too, had been a pianist and was as averse to publicity as Miss Shepherd ever was. When I first heard of her I felt somehow she was a rival and somehow disauthenticated the story of my lady in the van. That's absurd, though of one thing I'm sure: Miss Shepherd would not have been pleased.

Miss Shepherd was solipsistic to a degree and, in her persistent refusal to take into account the concerns or feelings of anyone else except herself and her inability to see the world and what happened in it except as it affected her, she behaved more like a man than a woman. I took this undeviating selfishness to have something to do with staying alive. Gratitude, humility, forgiveness or fellow feelings were foreign to her nature or had become so over the years, but had she been otherwise she might not have survived as long as she did. She hated noise, though she made plenty, particularly when sitting in her three-wheeler on a Sunday morning revving the engine to recharge the battery. She hated children. Reluctant to have the police called when the van's window had been broken and herself hurt, she would want the law summoning if there were children playing in the street and making what she considered too much noise or indeed any noise at all.

She inhabited a different world from ordinary humanity, a world in which the Virgin Mary would be encountered outside the Post Office in Parkway and Mr Khrushchev higher up the street; a world in which her advice was welcomed by world leaders and the College of Cardinals took note of her opinion. Seeing herself as the centre of the world, she had great faith in the power of the individual voice, even when it could only be heard through pamphlets photocopied at Prontaprint or read on the pavement outside Williams and Glyn's Bank.

I never questioned Miss Shepherd on the subject but what intrigued me about the regular appearances put in by the Virgin Mary was that she seldom turned up in her traditional habiliments; no sky-blue veil for her, still less a halo. Before leaving heaven for earth the BVM always seemed to go through the dressing-up box so that she could come down as Queen Victoria, say, or dressed in what sounded very much like a sari. And not only her. One of my father's posthumous appearances was as a Victorian statesman, and an old tramp, grey-haired and not undistinguished, was confidently identified as St Joseph (minus his donkey), just as I was taken briefly for St John.

With their fancy dress and a good deal of gliding about, it was hard not to find Miss Shepherd's visions comic, but they were evidence of a faith that manifestly sustained her and a component of her daily and difficult life. In one of her pamphlets she mentioned the poet Francis Thompson, who was a Catholic as she was (and who lived in similar squalor). Her vision of the intermingling of this world and the next was not unlike his:

> But (when so sad thou canst not sadder)
> Cry: – and upon thy so sore loss
> Shall shine the traffic of Jacob's ladder
> Pitched betwixt heaven and Charing Cross.
>
> Yea, in the night, my Soul, my daughter,
> Cry, – clinging Heaven by the hems;
> And lo, Christ walking on the water
> Not of Gennesareth, but Thames!

It's now over a quarter of a century since Miss Shepherd died, but hearing a van door slide shut will still take me back to the time when she was in the garden. For Marcel, the narrator in Proust's *Remembrance of Things Past*, the sound that took him back was that of the gate of his aunt's idyllic garden; with me it's the door of a broken-down Commer van. The discrepancy is depressing but then most writers discover quite early on that they're not going to be Proust. Besides, I couldn't have heard my own garden gate because in order to deaden the (to her) irritating noise Miss Shepherd had insisted on me putting a piece of chewing gum on the latch.

ALAN BENNETT, April 2015

THE LADY IN THE VAN

the original memoir by Alan Bennett

Good nature, or what is often considered as such, is the most selfish of all virtues: it is nine times out of ten mere indolence of disposition.

WILLIAM HAZLITT, 'On the Knowledge of Character' (1822)

'I ran into a snake this afternoon,' Miss Shepherd said. 'It was coming up Parkway. It was a long, grey snake — a boa constrictor possibly. It looked poisonous. It was keeping close to the wall and seemed to know its way. I've a feeling it may have been heading for the van.' I was relieved that on this occasion she didn't demand that I ring the police, as she regularly did if anything out of the ordinary occurred. Perhaps this was too out of the ordinary (though it turned out the pet shop in Parkway had been broken into the previous night, so she may have seen a snake). She brought her mug over and I made her a drink, which she took back to the van. 'I thought I'd better tell you,' she said, 'just to be on the safe side. I've had some close shaves with snakes.'

This encounter with the putative boa constrictor was in the summer of 1971, when Miss Shepherd and her van had for some months been at a permanent halt opposite my house in Camden Town. I had first come across her a few years previously, stood by her van, stalled as usual, near the convent at the top of the street. The convent (which was to have a subsequent career as the Japanese School) was a gaunt reformatory-like building that housed a dwindling garrison of aged nuns and was notable for a striking crucifix attached to the wall overlooking the traffic lights. There was something about the position of Christ, pressing himself against the grim pebbledash beneath the barred windows of the convent, that called up visions of the Stalag and the searchlight and which had caused us to dub him 'The Christ of Colditz'. Miss Shepherd, not looking un-crucified herself, was standing by her vehicle in an attitude with which I was to become very familiar, left arm extended with the palm flat against the side of the van indicating ownership, the right arm summoning anyone who was fool enough to take notice of her, on this occasion me. Nearly six foot, she was a commanding figure, and would have been more so had she not been kitted out in greasy raincoat, orange skirt, Ben Hogan golfing-cap and carpet slippers. She would be going on sixty at this time.

She must have prevailed on me to push the van as far as Albany Street, though I recall nothing of the exchange. What I do remember was being overtaken by two policemen in a panda car as I trundled the van across Gloucester Bridge; I thought that, as the van was certainly holding up the traffic, they might have lent a hand. They were wiser than I knew. The other feature of this first run-in with Miss Shepherd was her driving technique. Scarcely had I put my shoulder to the back of the van, an old Bedford, than a long arm was stretched elegantly out of the driver's window to indicate in textbook fashion that she (or rather I) was moving off. A few yards further on, as we were about to turn into Albany

Street, the arm emerged again, twirling elaborately in the air to indicate that we were branching left, the movement done with such boneless grace that this section of the Highway Code might have been choreographed by Petipa with Ulanova at the wheel. Her 'I am coming to a halt' was less poised, as she had plainly not expected me to give up pushing and shouted angrily back that it was the other end of Albany Street she wanted, a mile further on. But I had had enough by this time and left her there, with no thanks for my trouble. Far from it. She even climbed out of the van and came running after me, shouting that I had no business abandoning her, so that passers-by looked at me as if I had done some injury to this pathetic scarecrow. 'Some people!' I suppose I thought, feeling foolish that I'd been taken for a ride (or taken her for one) and cross that I'd fared worse than if I'd never lifted a finger, these mixed feelings to be the invariable aftermath of any transaction involving Miss Shepherd. One seldom was able to do her a good turn without some thoughts of strangulation.

It must have been a year or so after this, and so some time in the late sixties, that the van first appeared in Gloucester Crescent. In those days the street was still a bit of a mixture. Its large semi-detached villas had originally been built to house the Victorian middle class, then it had gone down in the world, and, though it had never entirely decayed, many of the villas degenerated into rooming-houses and so were among the earliest candidates for what is now called 'gentrification' but which was then called 'knocking through'. Young professional couples, many of them in journalism or television, bought up the houses, converted them and (an invariable feature of such conversions) knocked the basement rooms together to form a large kitchen/dining-room. In the mid-sixties I wrote a BBC TV series, *Life in NW1*, based on one such family, the Stringalongs, whom Mark Boxer then took over to people a cartoon strip in the *Listener*, and who kept cropping up in his drawings for the rest of his life. What made the social set-up funny was the disparity between the style in which the new arrivals found themselves able to live and their progressive opinions: guilt, put simply, which today's gentrifiers are said famously not to feel (or 'not to have a problem about'). We did have a problem, though I'm not sure we were any better for it. There was a gap between our social position and our social obligations. It was in this gap that Miss Shepherd (in her van) was able to live.

October 1969. When she is not in the van Miss S. spends much of her day sitting on the pavement in Parkway, where she has a pitch outside Williams & Glyn's Bank. She sells tracts, entitled 'True View: Mattering Things', which she writes herself, though this isn't something she will admit. 'I sell them, but so far as the authorship is concerned I'll say they are anonymous and that's as far as I'm prepared to go.' She generally chalks the gist of the current pamphlet on the pavement, though with no attempt at artistry. 'St Francis FLUNG money from him' is today's message, and prospective customers have to step over it to get into the bank. She also makes a few coppers selling pencils. 'A gentleman came the other day and said that the pencil he had bought from me was the best pencil on the market at the present time. It lasted him three months. He'll be back for another one shortly.' D., one of the more conventional neighbours (and not a knocker-through), stops me and says, 'Tell me, is she a *genuine* eccentric?'

April 1970. Today we moved the old lady's van. An obstruction order has been put under the windscreen wiper, stating that it was stationed outside number 63 and is a danger to public health. This order, Miss S. insists, is a statutory order: 'And statutory means standing – in this case standing outside number 63 – so, if the van is moved on, the order will be invalid.' Nobody ventures to argue with this, but she can't decide whether her next pitch should be outside number 61 or further on. Eventually she decides there is 'a nice space' outside 62 and plumps for that. My neighbour Nick Tomalin and I heave away at the back of the van, but while she is gracefully indicating that she is moving off (for all of the fifteen feet) the van doesn't budge. 'Have you let the handbrake off?' Nick Tomalin asks. There is a pause. 'I'm just in the process of taking it off.' As we are poised for the move, another Camden Town eccentric materialises, a tall, elderly figure in long overcoat and Homburg hat, with a distinguished grey moustache and in his buttonhole a flag for the Primrose League. He takes off a grubby canary glove and leans a shaking hand against the rear of the van (OLU 246), and when we have moved it forward the few statutory feet he puts on his glove again, saying, 'If you should need me I'm just round the corner' (i.e. in Arlington House, the working men's hostel).

I ask Miss S. how long she has had the van. 'Since 1965,' she says, 'though don't spread that around. I got it to put my things in. I came down from St Albans in it, and plan to go back there eventually. I'm just pedalling water at the moment. I've always been in the transport line. Chiefly delivery and chauffeuring. You know,' she says mysteriously – 'renovated army vehicles. And I've got good topography. I always have had. I knew Kensington in the blackout.'

This van (there were to be three others in the course of the next twenty years) was originally brown, but by the time it had reached the Crescent it had been given a coat of yellow. Miss S. was fond of yellow ('It's the papal colour') and was never content to leave her vehicles long in their original trim. Sooner or later she could be seen moving slowly round her immobile home, thoughtfully touching up the rust from a tiny tin of primrose paint, looking, in her long dress and sunhat, much as Vanessa Bell would have looked had she gone in for painting Bedford vans. Miss S. never appreciated the difference between car enamel and ordinary gloss paint, and even this she never bothered to mix. The result was that all her vehicles ended up looking as if they had been given a coat of badly made custard or plastered with scrambled egg. Still, there were few occasions on which one saw Miss Shepherd genuinely happy and one of them was when she was putting paint on. A few years before she died she went in for a Reliant Robin (to put more of her things in). It was actually yellow to start with, but that didn't save it from an additional coat, which she applied as Monet might have done, standing back to judge the effect of each brush-stroke. The Reliant stood outside my gate. It was towed away earlier this year, a scatter of yellow drops on the kerb all that remains to mark its final parking place.

January 1971. Charity in Gloucester Crescent takes refined forms. The publishers next door are bringing out some classical volume and to celebrate the event last night held a Roman dinner. This morning the au pair was to be seen knocking at the window of the van with a plate of Roman remains. But Miss S. is never easy to help. After twelve last night I saw her striding up the Crescent waving her stick and telling someone to be off. Then I heard a retreating middle-class voice say plaintively, 'But I only asked if you were all right.'

June 1971. Scarcely a day passes now without some sort of incident involving the old lady. Yesterday evening around ten a sports car swerves over to her side of the road so that the driver, rich, smart and in his twenties, can lean over and bang on the side of the van, presumably to flush out for his grinning girlfriend the old witch who lives there. I shout at him and he sounds his horn and roars off. Miss S. of course wants the police called, but I can't see the point, and indeed around five this morning I wake to find two policemen at much the same game, idly shining their torches in the windows in the hope that she'll wake up and enliven a dull hour of their beat. Tonight a white car reverses dramatically up the street, screeches to a halt beside the van, and a burly young man jumps out and gives the van a terrific shaking. Assuming (hoping, probably) he would have driven off by the time I get outside, I find he's still there, and ask him what the fuck he thinks he's doing. His response is quite mild. 'What's up with you then?' he asks. 'You still on the telly? You nervous? You're trembling all over.' He then calls me a fucking cunt and drives off. After all that, of course, Miss S. isn't in the van at all, so I end up as usual more furious with her than I am with the lout.

These attacks, I'm sure, disturbed my peace of mind more than they did hers. Living in the way she did, every day must have brought such cruelties. Some of the stallholders in the Inverness Street market used to persecute her with medieval relish – and children too, who both inflict and suffer such casual cruelties themselves. One night two drunks systematically smashed all the windows of the van, the flying glass cutting her face. Furious over any small liberty, she was only mildly disturbed by this. 'They may have had too much to drink by mistake,' she said. 'That does occur through not having eaten, possibly. I don't want a case.' She was far more interested in 'a ginger feller I saw in Parkway in company with Mr Khrushchev. Has he disappeared recently?'

But to find such sadism and intolerance so close at hand began actively to depress me, and having to be on the alert for every senseless attack made it impossible to work. There came a day when, after a long succession of such incidents, I suggested that she spend at least the nights in a lean-to at the side of my house. Initially reluctant, as with any change, over the next two years she gradually abandoned the van for the hut.

In giving her sanctuary in my garden and landing myself with a tenancy that went on eventually for fifteen years I was never under any illusion that the impulse was purely charitable. And of course it made me furious that I had been driven to such a pass. But I wanted a quiet life as much as, and possibly more than, she did. In the garden she was at least out of harm's way.

October 1973. I have run a lead out to the lean-to and now regularly have to mend Miss S.'s electric fire, which she keeps fusing by plugging too many appliances into the attachment. I sit on the steps fiddling with the fuse while she squats on her haunches in the hut. 'Aren't you cold? You could come in here. I could light a candle and then it would be a bit warmer. The toad's been in once or twice. He was in here with a slug. I think he may be in love with the slug. I tried to turn it out and it got very disturbed. I thought he was going to go for me.' She complains that there is not enough room in the shed and suggests I get her a tent, which she could then use to store some of her things. 'It would only be three feet high and by rights ought to be erected in a meadow. Then there are these shatterproof greenhouses. Or something could be done with old raincoats possibly.'

March 1974. The council are introducing parking restrictions in the Crescent. Residents' bays have been provided and yellow lines drawn up the rest of the street. To begin with, the workmen are very understanding, painting the yellow line as far as the van, then beginning again on the other side so that technically it is still legally parked. However, a higher official has now stepped in and served a removal order on it, so all this week there has been a great deal of activity as Miss S. transports cargoes of plastic bags across the road, through the garden and into the hut. While professing faith in divine protection for the van, she is prudently clearing out her belongings against its possible removal. A notice she has written declaring the council's action illegal twirls idly under the windscreen wiper.

'The notice was served on a Sunday. I believe you can serve search warrants on a Sunday but nothing else, possibly. I should have the Freedom of the Land for the good articles I've sold on the economy.' She is particularly concerned about the tyres of the van which 'may be miraculous. They've only been pumped up twice since 1964. If I get another vehicle'– and Lady W. is threatening to buy her one – 'I'd like them transferred.'

The old van was towed away in April 1974 and another one provided by Lady W. ('a titled Catholic lady', as Miss S. always referred to her). Happy to run to a new (albeit old) van, Lady W. was understandably not anxious to have it parked outside her front door and eventually, and perhaps by now inevitably, the van and Miss S. ended up in my garden. This van was roadworthy, and Miss S. insisted on being the one to drive it through the gate into the garden, a manoeuvre which once again enabled her to go through her full repertoire of hand signals. Once the van was on site Miss S. applied the handbrake with such determination that, like Excalibur, it could never thereafter be released, rusting so firmly into place that when the van came to be moved ten years later it had to be hoisted over the wall by the council crane.

This van (and its successor, bought in 1983) now occupied a paved area between my front door and the garden gate, the bonnet of the van hard by my front step, its rear door, which Miss S. always used to get in and out of, a few feet from the gate. Callers at the house had to squeeze past the back of the van and come down the side, and while they waited for my door to be opened they would be scrutinised from behind the murky windscreen

Miss Shepherd, *c.*1980 © *Tom Miller*

Maggie Smith © *Antony Crolla*

Maggie Smith, Nicholas Hytner, Alex Jennings *Photo: Nicola Dove*
    © *Van Productions*
Alex Jennings and Alan Bennett © *Antony Crolla*

Maggie Smith
Alex Jennings, Deborah Findlay, Roger Allam
© *Antony Crolla*

Cecilia Noble
Claire Foy
Alan Bennett and Gwen Taylor
© *Antony Crolla*

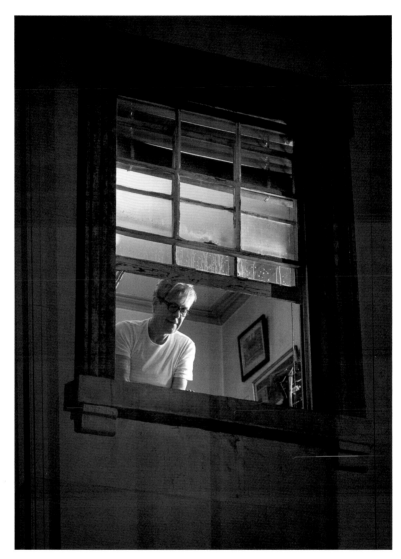

Alex Jennings © *Antony Crolla*

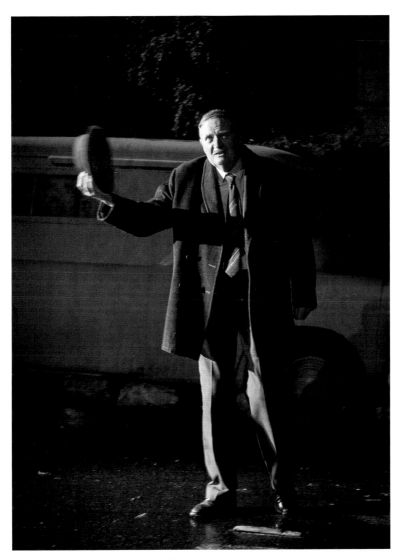

Jim Broadbent © *Antony Crolla*

Nicholas Burns, Richard Griffiths, Pandora Colin, Archie Surridge
Samuel Anderson
Frances de la Tour and Maggie Smith
© *Antony Crolla*

by Miss Shepherd. If they were unlucky, they would find the rear door open with Miss S. dangling her large white legs over the back. The interior of the van, a midden of old clothes, plastic bags and half-eaten food, was not easy to ignore, but should anyone Miss S. did not know venture to speak to her she would promptly tuck her legs back and wordlessly shut the door. For the first few years of her sojourn in the garden I would try and explain to mystified callers how this situation had arisen, but after a while I ceased to care, and when I didn't mention it nor did anyone else.

At night the impression was haunting. I had run a cable out from the house to give her light and heating, and through the ragged draperies that hung over the windows of the van a visitor would glimpse Miss S.'s spectral figure, often bent over in prayer or lying on her side like an effigy on a tomb, her face resting on one hand, listening to Radio 4. Did she hear any movements she would straightaway switch off the light and wait, like an animal that has been disturbed, until she was sure the coast was clear and could put the light on again. She retired early and would complain if anyone called or left late at night. On one occasion Coral Browne was coming away from the house with her husband, Vincent Price, and they were talking quietly. 'Pipe down,' snapped the voice from the van, 'I'm trying to sleep.' For someone who had brought terror to millions it was an unexpected taste of his own medicine.

December 1974. Miss S. has been explaining to me why the old Bedford (the van not the music-hall) ceased to go, 'possibly'. She had put in some of her home-made petrol, based on a recipe for petrol substitute she read about several years ago in a newspaper. 'It was a spoonful of petrol, a gallon of water and a pinch of something you could get in every High Street. Well, I got it into my head, I don't know why, that it was bicarbonate of soda, only I think I was mistaken. It must be either sodium chloride or sodium nitrate, only I've since been told sodium chloride is salt and the man in Boots wouldn't sell me the other, saying it might cause explosions. Though I think me being an older person he knew I would be more responsible. Though not all old ladies perhaps.'

February 1975. Miss S. rings, and when I open the door she makes a bee-line for the kitchen stairs. 'I'd like to see you. I've called several times. I wonder whether I can use the toilet first.' I say I think this is pushing it a bit. 'I'm not pushing it at all. I just will do the interview better if I can use the toilet first.' Afterwards she sits down in her green mac and purple headscarf, the knuckles of one large mottled hand resting on the clean, scrubbed table, and explains how she has devised a method of 'getting on the wireless'. I was to ask the BBC to give me a phone-in programme ('something someone like you could get put on in a jiffy') and then she would ring me up from the house. 'Either that or I could get on *Petticoat Line*. I know a darn sight more on moral matters than most of them. I could sing my song over the telephone. It's a lovely song, called "The End of the World"' (which is pure *Beyond the Fringe*). 'I won't commit myself to singing it – not at this moment – but I probably would. Some sense should be said and knowledge known. It could all be anonymous. I could be called The Lady Behind the Curtain. Or A Woman of Britain. You could take a nom-de-plume view of it.' This idea of The Woman Behind the Curtain has obviously taken her fancy and she begins to expand on it, demonstrating where the curtain could be, her side of it coincidentally taking in the television and the easy chair. She could be behind the curtain, she explains, do her periodic broadcasts, and the rest of the time 'be a guest at the television and take in some civilisation. Perhaps there would be gaps filled with nice classical music. I know one: "Prelude and Liebestraum" by Liszt. I believe he was a Catholic priest. It means "love's dream", only not the sexy stuff. It's the love of God and the sanctification of labour and so on, which would recommend it to celibates like you and me, possibly.' Shocked at this tentative bracketing of our conditions, I quickly get rid of her and, though it's a bitter cold night, open the windows wide to get rid of the smell.

The Woman Behind the Curtain remained a favourite project of hers, and in 1976 she wrote to Aiman (*sic*) Andrews: 'Now that *This is Your Life* is ended, having cost too much etc., I might be able to do a bit as The Lady Behind the Curtain. All you need do is put a curtain up to hide me but permit words of sense to come forth in answer to some questions. Sense is needed.' Hygiene was needed too, but possibly in an effort to persuade me about being behind the curtain she brought the subject up herself. 'I'm by nature a very clean person. I have a testimonial for a Clean Room, awarded me some years ago, and my aunt, herself spotless, said I was the cleanest of my mother's children, particularly in the unseen places.' I never fathomed her toilet arrangements. She only once asked me to buy her toilet rolls ('I use them to wipe my face'), but whatever happened in that department I took to be part of some complicated arrangement involving the plastic bags she used to hurl from the van every morning. When she could still manage stairs she did very occasionally use my loo, but I didn't encourage it; it was here, on the threshold of the toilet, that my charity stopped short. Once when I was having some building work done (and was, I suppose, conscious of what the workmen were thinking), I very boldly said there was a smell of urine. 'Well, what can you expect when they're raining bricks down on me all day? And then I think there's a mouse. So that would make a cheesy smell, possibly.'

Miss S.'s daily emergence from the van was highly dramatic. Suddenly and without warning the rear door would be flung open to reveal the tattered draperies that masked the terrible interior. There was a pause, then through the veils would be hurled several bulging plastic sacks. Another pause, before slowly and with great caution one sturdy slippered leg came feeling for the floor before the other followed and one had the first sight of the day's wardrobe. Hats were always a feature: a black railwayman's hat with a long neb worn slightly on the skew so that she looked like a drunken signalman or a French guardsman of the 1880s; there was her Charlie Brown pitcher's hat; and in June 1977 an octagonal straw table-mat, tied on with a chiffon scarf and a bit of cardboard for the peak. She also went in for green eyeshades. Her skirts had a telescopic appearance, as they had often been lengthened many times over by the simple expedient of sewing a strip of extra cloth around the hem, though with no attempt at matching. One skirt was made by sewing several orange dusters together. When she fell foul of authority she put it down to her clothes. Once, late at night, the police rang me from Tunbridge Wells. They had picked her up on the station, thinking her dress was a nightie. She was indignant. 'Does it look like a nightie? You see lots of people wearing dresses like this. I don't think this style can have got to Tunbridge Wells yet.'

Miss S. seldom wore stockings, and alternated between black pumps and brown carpet slippers. Her hands and feet were large, and she was what my grandmother would have called 'a big-boned woman'. She was middle class and spoke in a middle-class way, though her querulous and often resentful demeanour tended to obscure this; it wasn't a gentle or a genteel voice. Running through her vocabulary was a streak of schoolgirl slang. She wouldn't say she was tired, she was 'all done up'; petrol was 'juice'; and if she wasn't keen on doing something she'd say 'I'm darned if I will'. All her conversation was impregnated with the vocabulary of her peculiar brand of Catholic fanaticism ('the dire importance of justice deeds'). It was the language of the leaflets she wrote, the 'possibly' with which she ended so many of her sentences an echo of the 'Subject to the Roman Catholic Church in her rights etc.' with which she headed every leaflet.

May 1976. I have had some manure delivered for the garden and, since the manure heap is not far from the van, Miss S. is concerned that people passing might think the smell is coming from there. She wants me to put a notice on the gate to the effect that the smell is the manure, not her. I say no, without adding, as I could, that the manure actually smells much nicer.

I am working in the garden when Miss B., the social worker, comes with a boxful of clothes. Miss S. is reluctant to open the van door, as she is listening to *Any Answers*, but eventually she slides on her bottom to the door of the van and examines the clothes. She is unimpressed.

MISS S.: I only asked for one coat.

MISS B.: Well, I brought three just in case you wanted a change.

MISS S.: I haven't got room for three. Besides, I was planning to wash this coat in the near future. That makes four.

MISS B.: This is my old nursing mac.

MISS S.: I have a mac. Besides, green doesn't suit me. Have you got the stick?

MISS B.: No. That's being sent down. It had to be made specially.

MISS S.: Will it be long enough?

MISS B.: Yes. It's a special stick.

MISS S.: I don't want a special stick. I want an ordinary stick. Only longer. Does it have a rubber thing on it?

When Miss B. has gone, Miss S. sits at the door of the van slowly turning over the contents of the box like a chimpanzee, sniffing them and holding them up and muttering to herself.

June 1976. I am sitting on the steps mending my bike when Miss S. emerges for her evening stroll. 'I went to Devon on Saturday,' she said. 'On this frisbee.' I suppose she means freebie, a countrywide concession to pensioners that BR ran last weekend. 'Dawlish I went to. People very nice. The man over the loudspeaker called us

Ladies and Gentlemen, and so he should. There was one person shouted, only he wasn't one of us – the son of somebody, I think.' And almost for the first time ever she smiled, and said how they had all been bunched up trying to get into this one carriage, a great crowd, and how she had been hoisted up. 'It would have made a film,' she said. 'I thought of you.' And she stands there in her grimy raincoat, strands of lank grey hair escaping from under her headscarf. I am thankful people had been nice to her, and wonder what the carriage must have been like all that hot afternoon. She then tells me about a programme on Francis Thompson she'd heard on the wireless, how he had tried to become a priest but had felt he had failed in his vocation, and had become a tramp. Then, unusually, she told me a little of her own life, and how she tried to become a nun on two occasions, had undergone instruction as a novice, but was forced to give it up on account of ill-health, and that she had felt for many years that she had failed. But that this was wrong, and it was not a failure. 'If I could have had more modern clothes, longer sleep and better air, possibly, I would have made it.'

'A bit of a spree,' she called her trip to Dawlish. 'My spree.'

June 1977. On this the day of the Jubilee, Miss S. has stuck a paper Union Jack in the cracked back window of the van. It is the only one in the Crescent. Yesterday she was wearing a headscarf and pinned across the front of it a blue Spontex sponge fastened at each side with a large safety pin, the sponge meant to form some kind of peak against the (very watery) sun. It looked like a favour worn by a medieval knight, or a fillet to ward off evil spirits. Still, it was better than last week's effort, an Afrika Korps cap from Lawrence Corner: Miss Shepherd – Desert Fox.

September 1979. Miss S. shows me a photograph she has taken of herself in a cubicle at Waterloo. She is very low in the frame, her mouth pulled down, the photo looking as if it has been taken after death. She is very pleased with it. 'I don't take a good photograph usually. That's the only photograph I've seen looks anything like me.' She wants two copies making of it. I say that it would be easier for her to go back to Waterloo and do two more. No – that would 'take it out of her'. 'I had one taken in France once when I was twenty-one or twenty-two. Had to go into the next village for it. I came out cross-eyed. I saw someone else's photo on their bus-pass and she'd come out looking like a nigger. You don't want to come out like a nigger if you can help it, do you?'

June 1980. Miss S. has gone into her summer rig: a raincoat turned inside out, with brown canvas panels and a large label declaring it the Emerald Weatherproof. This is topped off with a lavender chiffon scarf tied round a sun visor made from an old cornflakes packet. She asks me to do her some shopping. 'I want a small packet of Eno's, some milk and some jelly babies. The jelly babies aren't urgent. Oh and, Mr Bennett, could you get me one of those little bottles of whisky? I believe Bell's is very good. I don't drink it – I just use it to rub on.'

August 1980. I am filming, and Miss S. sees me leaving early each morning and returning late. Tonight her scrawny hand comes out with a letter marked 'Please consider carefully':

An easier way for Mr Bennett to earn could be possibly with my co-operative part. Two young men could follow me in a car, one with a camera to get a funny film like Old Mother Riley Joins Up *possibly. If the car stalls they could then push it. Or they could go on the buses with her at a distance. Comedy happens without trying sometimes, or at least an interesting film covering a Senior Citizen's use of the buses can occur. One day to Hounslow, another to Reading or Heathrow. The bus people ought to be pleased, but it might need their permission. Then Mr Bennett could put his feet up more and rake it in, possibly.*

October 1980. Miss S. has started hankering after a caravan trailer and has just missed one she saw in *Exchange and Mart*: 'little net curtains all round, three bunks'. 'I wouldn't use them all, except,' she says ominously, 'to put things on. Nice little windows – £275. They said it was sold, only they may have thought I was just an old tramp . . . I was thinking of offering to help Mrs Thatcher with the economy. I wouldn't ask any money, as I'm on social security, so it would come cheap for her. I might ask her for some perks, though. Like a caravan. I would write to her but she's away. I know what's required. It's perfectly simple: Justice.'

No political party quite catered to Miss S.'s views, though the National Front came close. She was passionately anti-Communist, and as long ago as 1945 had written a letter to Jesus 'concerning the dreadful situation feared from the Yalta agreement'. The trouble was that her political opinions, while never moderate, were always tempered by her idiosyncratic view of the human physiognomy. Older was invariably wiser, which is fair if debatable, except that with Miss S. taller was wiser too. But height had its drawbacks, and it was perhaps because she was tall herself that she believed a person's height added to their burdens, put them under some strain. Hence, though she was in sympathy with Mr Heath on everything except the Common Market, 'I do think that Mr Wilson, personally, may have seen better in regard to Europe, being on the Opposition bench with less salary and being older, smaller and under less strain.' She was vehemently opposed to the Common Market – the 'common' always underlined when she wrote about it on the pavement, as if it were the sheer vulgarity of the economic union she particularly objected to. Never very lucid in her leaflets, she got especially confused over the EEC. 'Not long ago a soul wrote, or else was considering writing [she cannot recall as to which and it may have been something of either] that she disassociated from the Common Market entry and the injustices feared concerning it, or something like that.' 'Enoch', as she invariably called Mr Powell, had got it right, and she wrote him several letters telling him so, but in the absence of a wholly congenial party she founded her own, the Fidelis Party. 'It will be a party caring for Justice (and as such not needing opposition). Justice in the world today with its gigantic ignorant conduct requires the rule of a Good Dictator, possibly.'

Miss S. never regarded herself as being at the bottom of the social heap. That place was occupied by 'the desperate poor' – i.e.

those with no roof over their heads. She herself was 'a cut above those in dire need', and one of her responsibilities in society she saw as interceding for them and for those whose plight she thought Mrs Thatcher had overlooked. Could it be brought to her attention (and she wrote Mrs T. several letters on the subject), alleviation would surely follow.

Occasionally she would write letters to other public figures. In August 1978 it was to the College of Cardinals, then busy electing a Pope. 'Your Eminences. I would like to suggest humbly that an older Pope might be admirable. Height can count towards knowledge too probably.' However this older (and hopefully taller) Pope she was recommending might find the ceremony a bit of a trial, so, ever the expert on headgear, she suggests that 'at the Coronation there could be a not so heavy crown, of light plastic possibly or cardboard for instance.'

February 1981. Miss S. has flu, so I am doing her shopping. I wait every morning by the side window of the van and, with the dark interior and her grimy hand holding back the tattered purple curtain, it is as if I am at the confessional. The chief items this morning are ginger nuts ('very warming') and grape juice. 'I think this is what they must have been drinking at Cana,' she says as I hand her the bottle. 'Jesus wouldn't have wanted them rolling about drunk, and this is non-alcoholic. It wouldn't do for everyone, but in my opinion it's better than champagne.'

October 1981. The curtain is drawn aside this morning and Miss S., still in what I take to be her nightclothes, talks of 'the discernment of spirits' that enabled her to sense an angelic presence near her when she was ill. At an earlier period, when she had her pitch outside the bank, she had sensed a similar angelic presence, and now, having seen his campaign leaflet, who should this turn out to be, 'possibly', but Our Conservative Candidate Mr Pasley-Tyler. She embarks on a long disquisition on her well-worn theme of age in politics. Mrs Thatcher is too young and travels too much. Not like President Reagan. 'You wouldn't catch him making all those U-turns round Australia.'

January 1982. 'Do you see he's been found, that American soldier?' This is Colonel Dozo, kidnapped by the Red Brigade and found after a shoot-out in a flat in Padua. 'Yes, he's been found,' she says triumphantly, 'and I know who found him.' Thinking it unlikely she has an acquaintance in the Italian version of the SAS, I ask whom she means. 'St Anthony of course. The patron saint of lost things. St Anthony of Padua.' 'Well,' I want to say, 'he didn't have far to look.'

May 1982. As I am leaving for Yorkshire, Miss S.'s hand comes out like the Ancient Mariner's: do I know if there are any steps at Leeds station? 'Why?' I ask warily, thinking she may be having thoughts of camping on my other doorstep. It turns out she just wants somewhere to go for a ride, so I suggest Bristol. 'Yes, I've been to Bristol. On the way back I came through Bath. That looked nice. Some beautifully parked cars.' She then recalls driving her reconditioned army vehicles and taking them up to Derbyshire. 'I did it in the war,' she says. 'Actually I overdid it in the war,' and somehow that is the thin end of the wedge that has landed her up here, yearning for travel on this May morning forty years later.

'Land' is a word Miss S. prefers to 'country'. 'This land . . .' Used in this sense, it's part of the rhetoric if not of madness at any rate of obsession. Jehovah's Witnesses talk of 'this land', and the National Front. Land is country plus destiny – country in the sight of God. Mrs Thatcher talks of 'this land'.

February 1983. A. telephones me in Yorkshire to say that the basement is under three inches of water, the boiler having burst. When told that the basement has been flooded, Miss S.'s only comment is 'What a waste of water'.

April 1983. 'I've been having bad nights,' says Miss S., 'but if I were elected I might have better nights.' She wants me to get her nomination papers so that she can stand for Parliament in the coming election. She would be the Fidelis Party candidate. The party, never very numerous, is now considerably reduced. Once she could count on five votes but now there are only two, one of whom is me, and I don't like to tell her I'm in the SDP. Still, I promise to write to the town hall for nomination papers. 'There's no kitty as yet,' she says, 'and I wouldn't want to do any of the meeting people. I'd be no good at that. The secretaries can do that (you get expenses). But I'd be very good at voting – better than they are, probably.'

May 1983. Miss S. asks me to witness her signature on the nomination form. 'I'm signing,' she says: 'are you witnessing?' She has approached various nuns to be her nominees. 'One sister I know would have signed but I haven't seen her for some years and she's got rather confused in the interim. I don't know what I'll do about leaflets. It would have to be an economy job – I couldn't run to the expense. Maybe I'll just write my manifesto on the pavement; that goes round like wildfire.'

May 1983. Miss S. has received her nomination papers. 'What should I describe myself as?' she asks through the window slit. 'I thought Elderly Spinster, possibly. It also says Title. Well my title is' – and she laughs one of her rare laughs – 'Mrs Shepherd. That's what some people call me out of politeness. And I don't deny it. Mother Teresa always says she's married to God. I could say I was married to the Good Shepherd, and that's what it's to do with, Parliament, looking after the flock. When I'm elected, do you think I shall have to live in Downing Street or could I run things from the van?'

I speak to her later in the day and the nomination business is beginning to get her down. 'Do you know anything about the Act of 1974? It refers to disqualifications under it. Anyway, it's all giving me a headache. I think there may be another election soon after this one, so it'll have been good preparation anyway.'

June 1984. Miss S. has been looking in *Exchange and Mart* again and has answered an advert for a white Morris Minor. 'It's the kind of car I'm used to – or I used to be used to. I feel the need to be mobile.' I raise the matter of a licence and insurance, which she always treats as tiresome formalities. 'What you don't understand is that I am insured. I am insured in heaven.' She claims that since she had been insured in heaven there has not been a scratch on the van. I point out that this is less to do with the celestial insurance than with the fact that the van is parked the whole time in my garden. She concedes that when she was on the road the van did used to get the occasional knock. 'Somebody came up behind me once and scratched the van. I wanted him to pay something – half-a-crown I think it was. He wouldn't.'

October 1984. Some new staircarpet fitted today. Spotting the old carpet being thrown out, Miss S. says it would be just the thing to put on the roof of the van to deaden the sound of rain. This exchange comes just as I am leaving for work, but I say that I do not want the van festooned with bits of old carpet – it looks bad enough as it is. When I come back in the evening I find half the carpet remnants slung over the roof. I ask Miss S. who has put them there, as she can't have done it herself. 'A friend,' she says mysteriously. 'A well-wisher.' Enraged, I pull down a token piece but the majority of it stays put.

April 1985. Miss S. has written to Mrs Thatcher applying for a post in 'the Ministry of Transport advisory, to do with drink and driving and that'. She also shows me the text of a letter she is pro-posing to send to the Argentinian Embassy on behalf of General Galtieri. 'What he doesn't understand is that Mrs Thatcher isn't the Iron Lady. It's me.'

To Someone in Charge of Argentina. 19 April 1985

Dear Sir,

*I am writing to help mercy towards the poor general who led your
forces in the war actually as a person of true knowledge more than might
be. I was concerned with Justice, Love and, in a manner of speaking, I was
in the war, as it were, shaking hands with your then leader, welcoming
him in spirit (it may have been to do with love of Catholic education for
Malvinas for instance) greatly meaning kindly negotiators etc. ... but I
fear that he may have thought it was Mrs Thatcher welcoming him in
that way and it may hence have unduly influenced him.*

*Therefore I beg you to have mercy on him indeed. Let him go,
reinstate him, if feasible. You may read publicly this letter if you wish to
explain mercy etc.*

I remain.

> *Yours truly*
>> *A Member of the Fidelis Party*
>> *(Servants of Justice)*

P.S. Others may have contributed to undue influence also.
P.P.S. Possibly without realising it.
Translate into Argentinian if you shd wish.

Sometime in 1980 Miss S. acquired a car, but before she'd managed
to have more than a jaunt or two in it ('It's a real goer!') it was
stolen and later found stripped and abandoned in the basement
of the council flats in Maiden Lane. I went to collect what was
left ('though the police may require it for evidence, possibly') and

found that even in the short time she'd had the Mini she'd managed to stuff it with the usual quota of plastic bags, kitchen rolls and old blankets, all plentifully doused in talcum powder. When she got a Reliant Robin in 1984 it was much the same, a second wardrobe as much as a second car. Miss Shepherd could afford to splash out on these vehicles because being parked in the garden meant that she had a permanent address, and so qualified for full social security and its various allowances. Since her only outgoings were on food, she was able to put by something and had an account in the Halifax and quite a few savings certificates. Indeed I heard people passing say, 'You know she's a millionaire,' the inference being no one in their right mind would let her live there if she weren't.

Her Reliant saw more action than the Mini, and she would tootle off in it on a Sunday morning, park on Primrose Hill ('The air is better'), and even got as far as Hounslow. More often than not, though, she was happy (and I think she was happy then) just to sit in the Reliant and rev the engine. However, since she generally chose to do this first thing on Sunday morning, it didn't endear her to the neighbours. Besides, what she described as 'a lifetime with motors' had failed to teach her was that revving a car does not charge the battery, so that when it regularly ran down I had to take it out and recharge it, knowing full well this would just mean more revving. ('No,' she insisted, 'I may be going to Cornwall next week, possibly.') This recharging of the battery wasn't really the issue: I was just ashamed to be seen delving under the bonnet of such a joke car.

March 1987. The nuns up the road – or, as Miss S. always refers to them, 'the sisters' – have taken to doing some of her shopping.

One of them leaves a bag on the back step of the van this morning. There are the inevitable ginger nuts, and several packets of sanitary towels. I can see these would be difficult articles for her to ask me to get, though to ask a nun to get them would seem quite hard for her too. They form some part of her elaborate toilet arrangements, and are occasionally to be seen laid drying across the soup-encrusted electric ring. As the postman says this morning, 'The smell sometimes knocks you back a bit.'

May 1987. Miss S. wants to spread a blanket over the roof (in addition to the bit of carpet) in order to deaden the sound of the rain. I point out that within a few weeks it will be dank and disgusting. 'No,' she says, '– weather-beaten.'

She has put a Conservative poster in the side window of the van. The only person who can see it is me.

This morning she was sitting at the open door of the van and as I edge by she chucks out an empty packet of Ariel. The blanket hanging over the pushchair is covered in washing powder. 'Have you spilt it?' I enquire. 'No,' she says crossly, irritated at having to explain the obvious. 'That's washing powder. When it rains, the blanket will get washed.' As I work at my table now I can see her bending over the pushchair, picking at bits of soap flakes and redistributing them over the blanket. No rain is at the moment forecast.

June 1987. Miss S. has persuaded the social services to allocate her a wheelchair, though what she's really set her heart on is the electric version.

MISS S.: That boy over the road has one. Why not me?

ME: He can't walk.

MISS S.: How does he know? He hasn't tried.

ME: Miss Shepherd, he has spina bifida.

MISS S.: Well, I was round-shouldered as a child. That may not be serious now, but it was quite serious then. I've gone through two wars, an infant in the first and not on full rations, in the ambulances in the second, besides being failed by the ATS. Why should old people be disregarded?

Thwarted in her ambition for a powered chair, Miss S. compensated by acquiring (I never found out where from) a second wheelchair ('in case the other conks out, possibly'). The full inventory of her wheeled vehicles now read: one van; one Reliant Robin; two wheelchairs; one folding pushchair; one folding (two-seater) pushchair. Now and again I would thin out the pushchairs by smuggling one onto a skip. She would put down this disappearance to children (never a favourite), and the number would shortly be made up by yet another wheelie from Reg's junk stall. Miss S. never mastered the technique of self-propulsion in the wheelchair because she refused to use the inner handwheel ('I can't be doing with all that silliness'). Instead, she preferred to punt herself along with two walking sticks, looking in the process rather like a skier on the flat. Eventually I had to remove the handwheel ('The extra weight affects my health').

July 1987. Miss S. (bright green visor, purple skirt, brown cardigan, turquoise fluorescent ankle socks) punts her way out through the gate in the wheelchair in a complicated manoeuvre which would be much simplified did she just push the chair out, as well she can. A passer-by takes pity on her, and she is whisked down to the market. Except not quite whisked, because the journey is made more difficult than need be by Miss S.'s refusal to take her feet off the ground, so the Good Samaritan finds himself pushing a wheelchair continually slurred and braked by these large, trailing, carpet-slippered feet. Her legs are so thin now the feet are as slack and flat as those of a camel.

Still, there will be one moment to relish on this, as on all these journeys. When she had been pushed back from the market, she will tell (and it is tell: there is never any thanks) whoever is pushing the chair to leave her opposite the gate but on the crown of the road. Then, when she thinks no one is looking, she lifts her feet, pushes herself off, and freewheels the few yards down to the gate. The look on her face is one of pure pleasure.

October 1987. I have been filming abroad. 'When you were in Yugoslavia,' asks Miss S., 'did you come across the Virgin Mary?' 'No,' I say, 'I don't think so.' 'Oh, well, she's appearing there. She's been appearing there every day for several years.' It's as if I've missed the major tourist attraction.

January 1988. I ask Miss S. if it was her birthday yesterday. She agrees guardedly. 'So you're seventy-seven.' 'Yes. How did you know?' 'I saw it once when you filled out the census form.' I give her a bottle of whisky, explaining that it's just to rub on. 'Oh. Thank you.' Pause. 'Mr Bennett. Don't tell anybody.' 'About the whisky?' 'No. About my birthday.' Pause. 'Mr Bennett.' 'Yes?' 'About the whisky either.'

March 1988. 'I've been doing a bit of spring cleaning,' says Miss S., kneeling in front of a Kienholz-like tableau of filth and decay. She says she has been discussing the possibility of a bungalow with the social worker, to which she would be prepared to contribute 'a few hundred or so'. It's possible that the bungalow might be made of asbestos, 'but I could wear a mask. I wouldn't mind that, and of course it would be much better from the fire point of view.' Hands in mittens made from old socks, a sanitary towel drying over the ring, and a glossy leaflet from the Halifax offering 'fabulous investment opportunities'.

April 1988. Miss S. asks me to get Tom M. to take a photograph of her for her new bus-pass. 'That would make a comedy, you know – sitting on a bus and your bus-pass out of date. You could make a fortune out of that with very little work involved, possibly. I was a born tragedian,' she says, 'or a comedian possibly. One or the other anyway. But I didn't realise it at the time. Big feet.' She pushes out her red, unstockinged ankles. 'Big hands.' The fingers stained brown. 'Tall. People trip over me. That's comedy. I wish they didn't, of course. I'd like it easier, but there it is. I'm not suggesting you do it,' she says hastily, feeling perhaps she's come too near self-revelation, 'only it might make people laugh.' All of this is said with a straight face and no hint of a smile, sitting in the wheelchair with her hands pressed between her knees and her baseball cap on.

May 1988. Miss S. sits in her wheelchair in the road, paintpot in hand, dabbing at the bodywork of the Reliant, which she will shortly enter, start, and rev for a contented half-hour before switching off and paddling down the road in her wheelchair. She has been nattering at Tom M. to mend the clutch, but there are conditions. It mustn't be on Sunday, which is the feast of St Peter and St Paul and a day of obligation. Nor can it be the following Sunday apparently, through the Feast of the Assumption falling on the Monday and being transferred back to the previous day. Amid all the chaos of her life and now, I think, more or less incontinent, she trips with fanatical precision through this liturgical minefield.

September 1988. Miss S. has started thinking about a flat again, though not the one the council offered her a few years ago. This time she has her eye on something much closer to home. My home. We had been talking outside, and I left her sitting on the step in the hall while I came back to work. This is often what happens: me sitting at my table, wanting to get on, Miss S. sitting outside rambling. This time she goes on talking about the flat, soliloquising almost, but knowing that I can hear. 'It need only be a little flat, even a room possibly. Of course, I can't manage stairs, so it would have to be on the ground floor. Though I'd pay to have a lift put in.' (Louder.) 'And the lift wouldn't be wasted. They'd have it for their old age. And they'll have to be thinking about their old age quite soon.' The tone of it is somehow familiar from years ago. Then I realise it's like one of the meant-to-be-overheard soliloquies of Richmal Crompton's William.

Her outfit this morning: orange skirt, made out of three or

four large dusters; a striped blue satin jacket; a green headscarf – blue eyeshield topped off by a khaki peaked cap with a skull-and-crossbones badge and Rambo across the peak.

February 1989. Miss S.'s religion is an odd mixture of traditional faith and a belief in the power of positive thinking. This morning, as ever, the Reliant battery is running low and she asks me to fix it. The usual argument takes place:

ME: Well, of course it's run down. It will run down unless you run the car. Revving up doesn't charge it. The wheels have to go round.

MISS S.: Stop talking like that. This car is not the same. There are miracles. There is faith. Negative thoughts don't help. (*She presses the starter again and it coughs weakly.*) There, you see. The devil's heard you. You shouldn't say negative things.

The interior of the van now indescribable.

March 1989. Miss S. sits in the wheelchair trying to open the sneck of the gate with her walking-stick. She tries it with one end, then reverses the stick and tries with the other. Sitting at my table, trying to work, I watch her idly, much as one would watch an ant trying to get round some obstacle. Now she bangs on the gate to attract the attention of a passer-by. Now she is wailing. Banging and wailing. I go out. She stops wailing, and explains she has her washing to do. As I manoeuvre her through the gate, I ask her if she's fit to go. Yes, only she will need help. I explain that I can't push her there. (Why can't I?) No, she doesn't want that. Would I just push her as far as the corner? I do so. Would I just push her a bit further? I explain that I can't take her to the launderette. (And anyway there is no launderette any more, so which launderette is she going to?) Eventually, feeling like Fletcher Christian (only not Christian) abandoning Captain Bligh, I leave her in the wheelchair outside Mary H.'s. Someone will come along. I would be more ashamed if I did not feel, even when she is poorly, that she knows exactly what she's about.

March 1989. There is a thin layer of talcum powder around the back door of the van and odd bits of screwed-up tissues smeared with what may or may not be shit, though there is no doubt about the main item of litter, which is a stained incontinence pad. My method of retrieving these items would not be unfamiliar at Sellafield. I don rubber gloves, put each hand inside a plastic bag as an additional protection, then, having swept the faecal artefacts together, gingerly pick them up and put them in the bin. 'Those aren't all my rubbish,' comes a voice from the van. 'Some of them blow in under the gate.'

April 1989. Miss S. has asked me to telephone the social services, and I tell her that a social worker will be calling. 'What time?' 'I don't know. But you're not going to be out. You haven't been out for a week.' 'I might be. Miracles do happen. Besides, she may not be able to talk to me. I may not be at the door end of the van. I might be at the other end.' 'So she can talk to you there.' 'And what if I'm in the middle?'

Miss C. thinks her heart is failing. She calls her Mary. I find this strange, though it is of course her name.

April 1989. A staple of Miss S.'s shopping-list these days is sherbet lemons. I have a stock of them in the house, but she insists I invest in yet more so that a perpetual supply of sherbet lemons may never be in doubt. 'I'm on them now. I don't want to have to go off them.'

I ask her if she would like a cup of coffee. 'Well, I wouldn't want you to go to all that trouble. I'll just have half a cup.'

Towards the end of her life Miss S. was befriended by an ex-nurse who lived locally. She put me in touch with a day centre who agreed to take Miss Shepherd in, give her a bath and a medical examination and even a bed in a single room where she could stay if she wanted. In retrospect I see I should have done something on the same lines years before, except that it was only when age and illness had weakened Miss Shepherd that she would accept such help. Even then it was not easy.

27 April 1989. A red ambulance calls to take Miss S. to the day centre. Miss B. talks to her for a while in the van, gradually coaxing her out and into the wheelchair, shit streaks over her swollen feet, a piece of toilet roll clinging to one scaly ankle. 'And if I don't like it,' she keeps asking, 'can I come back?' I reassure her, but, looking at the inside of the van and trying to cope with the stench, I find it hard to see how she can go on living here much longer. Once she sees the room they are offering her, the bath, the clean sheets, I can't imagine her wanting to come back. And indeed she makes more fuss than usual about locking the van door, which suggests she accepts that she may not be returning. I note how, with none of my distaste, the ambulance driver bends over her as he puts her on the hoist, his careful rearrangement of her greasy clothing, pulling her skirt down over her knees in the interests of modesty. The chair goes on the hoist, and slowly she rises and comes into view above the level of the garden wall and is wheeled into the ambulance. There is a certain distinction about her as she leaves, a Dorothy Hodgkin of vagabonds, a derelict Nobel Prize-winner, the heavy folds of her grimy face set in a kind of resigned satisfaction. She may even be enjoying herself.

When she has gone I walk round the van noting the occasions of our battle: the carpet tiles she managed to smuggle on to the roof, the blanket strapped on to muffle the sound of the rain, the black bags under the van stuffed with her old clothes – sites of skirmishes all of which I'd lost. Now I imagine her bathed and bandaged and cleanly clothed and starting a new life. I even see myself visiting and taking flowers.

This fantasy rapidly fades when around 2.30 Miss S. reappears, washed and in clean clothes, it's true, and with a long pair of white hospital socks over her shrunken legs, but obviously very pleased to be back. She has a telephone number where her new friends can be contacted, and she gives it to me. 'They can be reached,' she says, 'any time – even over the holiday. They're on a long-distance bleep.'

As I am leaving for the theatre, she bangs on the door of the van with her stick. I open the door. She is lying wrapped in clean white sheets on a quilt laid over all the accumulated filth and rubbish of the van. She is still worrying that I will have her taken to hospital. I tell her there's no question of it and that she can stay as long as she wants. I close the door, but there is another bang and I reassure her again. Once more I close the door, but she bangs again. 'Mr Bennett.' I have to strain to hear. 'I'm sorry the van's in such a state. I haven't been able to do any spring cleaning.'

28 April. I am working at my table when I see Miss B. arrive with a pile of clean clothes for Miss Shepherd, which must have been washed for her at the day centre yesterday. Miss B. knocks at the door of the van, then opens it, looks inside and – something nobody has ever done before – gets in. It's only a moment before she comes out, and I know what has happened before she rings the bell. We go back to the van where Miss Shepherd is dead, lying on her left side, flesh cold, face gaunt, the neck stretched out as if for the block, and a bee buzzing round her body.

It is a beautiful day, with the garden glittering in the sunshine, strong shadows by the nettles, and bluebells out under the wall, and I remember how in her occasional moments of contemplation she would sit in the wheelchair and gaze at the garden. I am filled with remorse for my harsh conduct towards her, though I know at the same time that it was not harsh. But still I never quite believed or chose to believe she was as ill as she was, and I regret too all the questions I never asked her. Not that she would have answered them. I have a strong impulse to stand at the gate and tell anyone who passes.

Miss B. meanwhile goes off and returns with a nice doctor from St Pancras who seems scarcely out of her teens. She gets into the van, takes the pulse in Miss S.'s outstretched neck, checks her with a stethoscope and, to save an autopsy, certifies death as from heart failure. Then comes the priest to bless her before she is taken to the funeral parlour, and he, too, gets into the van – the third person to do so this morning, and all of them without distaste or ado in what to me seem three small acts of heroism. Stooping over the body, his bright white hair brushing the top of the van, the priest murmurs an inaudible prayer and makes a cross on Miss S.'s hands and head. Then they all go off and I come inside to wait for the undertakers.

I have been sitting at my table for ten minutes before I realise that the undertakers have been here all the time, and that death nowadays comes (or goes) in a grey Ford transit van that is standing outside the gate. There are three undertakers, two young and burly, the third older and more experienced – a sergeant, as it were, and two corporals. They bring out a rough grey-painted coffin, like a prop a conjuror might use, and, making no comment on the surely extraordinary circumstances in which they find it, put a sheet of white plastic bin-liner over the body and manhandle it into their magic box, where it falls with a bit of a thud. Across the road, office workers stroll down from the Piano Factory for their lunch, but nobody stops or even looks much, and the Asian woman who has to wait while the box is carried over the pavement and put in the (other) van doesn't give it a backward glance.

Later I go round to the undertakers to arrange the funeral, and the manager apologises for their response when I had originally phoned. A woman had answered, saying, 'What exactly is it you want?' Not thinking callers rang undertakers with a great variety of requests, I was nonplussed. Then she said briskly, 'Do you want someone taking away?' The undertaker explains that her seemingly unhelpful manner was because she thought my call wasn't genuine. 'We get so many hoaxes these days. I've often gone round to collect a corpse only to have it open the door.'

9 May. Miss Shepherd's funeral is at Our Lady of Hal, the Catholic church round the corner. The service has been slotted into the ten o'clock mass, so that, in addition to a contingent of neighbours, the congregation includes what I take to be regulars: the fat little man in thick glasses and trainers who hobbles along to the church every day from Arlington House; several nuns, among them the ninety-nine-year-old sister who was in charge when Miss S. was briefly a novice; a woman in a green straw hat like an upturned plant pot who eats toffees throughout; and another lady who plays the harmonium in tan slacks and a tea-cosy wig. The server, a middle-aged man with white hair, doesn't wear a surplice, just ordinary clothes with an open-necked shirt, and, but for knowing all the sacred drill, might have been roped in from the group on the corner outside The Good Mixer. The priest is a young Irish boy with a big, red peasant face and sandy hair, and he, too, stripped of his cream-coloured cassock, could be wielding a pneumatic drill in the roadworks outside. I keep thinking about these characters during the terrible service, and it reinforces what I have always known: that I could never be a Catholic because I'm such a snob, and that the biggest sacrifice Newman made when he turned his back on the C of E was the social one.

Yet kindness abounds. In front of us is a thin old man who knows the service backwards, and seeing we have no prayer books he lays down his own on top of his copy of the *Sun*, goes

back up the aisle to fetch us some, and hands them round, all
the time saying the responses without faltering. The first hymn
is Newman's 'Lead Kindly Light', which I try and sing, while
making no attempt at the second hymn, which is 'Kum Ba Ya'.
The priest turns out to have a good strong voice, though its tone
is more suited to 'Kum Ba Ya' than to Newman and J. B. Dykes.
The service itself is wet and wandering, even more so than the
current Anglican equivalent, though occasionally one catches in
the watered-down language a distant echo of 1662. Now, though,
arrives the bit I dread, the celebration of fellowship, which always
reminds me of the warm-up Ned Sherrin insisted on inflicting
on the studio audience before *Not So Much a Programme*, when
everyone had to shake hands with their neighbour. But again the
nice man who fetched us the prayer books shames me when he
turns round without any fuss or embarrassment and smilingly
shakes my hand. Then it is the mass proper, the priest distributing
the wafers to the ninety-nine-year-old nun and the lady with the
plant pot on her head, as Miss S. lies in her coffin at his elbow.
Finally there is another hymn, this one by the (to me) unknown
hymnodist Kevin Norton, who's obviously reworked it from his
unsuccessful entry for the Eurovision Song Contest; and with the
young priest acting as lead singer, and the congregation a rather
subdued backing group, Miss Shepherd is carried out.

The neighbours, who are not quite mourners, wait on the
pavement outside as the coffin is hoisted onto the hearse. 'A cut
above her previous vehicle,' remarks Colin H.; and comedy persists
when the car accompanying the hearse to the cemetery refuses to
start. It's a familiar scene, and one which I've played many times,

with Miss S. waiting inside her vehicle as wellwishers lift the bonnet, fetch leads and give it a jump start. Except this time she's dead.

Only A. and I and Clare, the ex-nurse who lately befriended Miss S., accompany the body, swept around Hampstead Heath at a less than funereal pace, down Bishop's Avenue and up to the St Pancras Cemetery, green and lush this warm, sunny day. We drive beyond the scattered woods to the furthest edge where stand long lines of new gravestones, mostly in black polished granite. Appropriately, in view of her lifelong love of the car, Miss S. is being buried within sight and sound of the North Circular Road, one carriageway the other side of the hedge, with juggernauts drowning the words of the priest as he commits the body to the earth. He gives us each a go with his little plastic bottle of holy water, we throw some soil into the grave, and then everybody leaves me to whatever solitary thoughts I might have, which are not many, before we are driven back to Camden Town – life reasserted when the undertaker drops us handily outside Sainsbury's.

In the interval between Miss Shepherd's death and her funeral ten days later I found out more about her life than I had in twenty years. She had indeed driven ambulances during the war, and was either blown up or narrowly escaped death when a bomb exploded nearby. I'm not sure that her eccentricity can be put down to this any more than to the legend, mentioned by one of the nuns, that it was the death of her fiancé in this incident that 'tipped her over'. It would be comforting to think that it is love, or the death of it, that imbalances the mind, but I think her early attempts to become a nun and her repeated failures ('too argumentative', one of the sisters said) point to a personality that must already have been quite awkward when she was a girl. After the war she spent some time in mental hospitals, but regularly absconded, finally remaining at large long enough to establish her competence to live unsupervised.

The turning-point in her life came when, through no fault of hers, a motorcyclist crashed into the side of her van. If her other vans were any guide, this one too would only have been insured in heaven, so it's not surprising she left the scene of the accident ('skedaddled', she would have said) without giving her name or address. The motorcyclist subsequently died, so that, while blameless in the accident, by leaving the scene of it she had committed a criminal offence. The police mounted a search for her. Having already changed her first name when she became a novice, now under very different circumstances she changed her second and, calling herself Shepherd, made her way back to Camden Town and the vicinity of the convent where she had taken her vows. And though in the years to come she had little to do with the nuns, or they with her, she was never to stray far from the convent for the rest of her life.

All this I learned in those last few days. It was as if she had been a character in Dickens whose history has to be revealed and her secrets told in the general setting-to-rights before the happy-ever-after, though all that this amounted to was that at long last I could bring my car into the garden to stand now where the van stood all those years.

THE LADY IN THE VAN:
The Film

CAST AND CREDITS

Cast in order of appearance

MISS SHEPHERD	Maggie Smith
UNDERWOOD	Jim Broadbent
YOUNG MARGARET FAIRCHILD	Clare Hammond
CONDUCTOR	George Fenton
BRITISH SYMPHONY ORCHESTRA	BBC Concert Orchestra
ALAN BENNETT	Alex Jennings
ESTATE AGENT	Jamie Parker
PAULINE	Deborah Findlay
RUFUS	Roger Allam
SAM PERRY	Richard Griffiths
FIONA PERRY	Pandora Colin
GILES PERRY	Nicholas Burns
ACTOR	Dominic Cooper
PASSER-BY	Giles Cooper
TOM PERRY	Tom Klenerman
MAM	Gwen Taylor
MRS VAUGHAN WILLIAMS	Frances de la Tour
LOIS, SOCIAL WORKER	Claire Foy
MARKET TRADER	James Corden
POLICEMAN	George Taylor
LEO FAIRCHILD	David Calder
INTERVIEWER	Eleanor Matsuura
LADY WIGGIN	Selina Cadell
MEN SHAKING VAN	Charlie Hancock
	Dan Raza

PRIEST	Dermot Crowley
MAN IN CONFESSIONAL	Clive Merrison
OUT OF WORK ACTOR	Samuel Barnett
YOUNG MAN WITH EARRING	Russell Tovey
JEHOVAH'S WITNESSES	Samuel Anderson
	Michelle Reid
ANOTHER YOUNG MAN	Sam Spruell
OLD NUN	Rosalind Knight
THEATRE DIRECTOR	Elliot Levey
STAGE MANAGER	Sarah Lieberson
MISS BRISCOE, SOCIAL WORKER	Cecilia Noble
BROADSTAIRS PIANIST	Hannah Watson
EDITH FAIRCHILD	Linda Broughton
DOCTOR AT OLD PEOPLE'S HOME	Stephen Campbell Moore
HOUSEKEEPER AT CONVENT	Marion Bailey
DR AT GLOUCESTER CRESCENT	Sacha Dhawan
AMBULANCE MAN	Andrew Knott
DAY CARE CENTRE WORKER	Lorna Brown
WOMAN IN DAY CENTRE	June Watson
BIKER	Sam McCardle
GOD	Tony Van Silva
ALAN'S PARTNER	Geoffrey Streatfield
ALAN BENNETT (2014)	Alan Bennett
Director	Nicholas Hytner
Screenplay by	Alan Bennett, from his memoir
Produced by	Kevin Loader, Nicholas Hytner, Damian Jones
Executive Producers	Christine Langan, Ed Wethered, Charles Moore, Miles Ketley
Director of Photography	Andrew Dunn, BSC
Production Designer	John Beard

Editor	Tariq Anwar
Music by	George Fenton
Line Producer	Faiza Hosenie
Costume Designer	Natalie Ward
Hair and Make-up Designer	Naomi Donne
Casting by	Toby Whale, CDG
Post Production Supervisor	Louise Seymour

The sound of squealing brakes, then a car crash.

Fade in:

EXT. COUNTRY ROAD. DAY

A country lane c. 1960 with Miss Shepherd at the wheel of a van barrelling along, her face set and anxious. Distantly we hear the sound of a police siren (or bell it would be in 1960). She pulls the van into a side road or clearing and waits, ducking behind the seat as she sees the police car pass the end of the road. Miss Shepherd rights herself, checks the side of the van. Wipes her hand on it. Blood. She crosses herself. Then starts up the van and drives off the way she has come.

As she turns the corner, we see that the police car has stopped at the end of the road. A solitary policeman, Underwood, gets out of the car and watches the van disappear.

Roll titles over:

INT. CONCERT HALL. NIGHT

A glamorous pianist in a décolleté evening gown (along the lines of Ann Todd in The Seventh Veil, *c. 1947) playing some bravura piano concerto.*

As the titles end, so does the concerto, and we hear Alan Bennett in voice-over and cut to:

INT. 23 GLOUCESTER CRESCENT. STUDY. DAY

Alan Bennett at his desk, writing.

ALAN BENNETT
(*voice-over*)

The smell is sweet, with urine only a minor component,
the prevalent odour suggesting the inside of someone's ear.
Dank clothes are there too, wet wool and onions, which
she eats raw, plus what for me has always been the essence
of poverty, damp newspaper.

*The sound of the lavatory flushing. Alan Bennett looks towards the
toilet door.*

Miss Shepherd's multi-flavoured aroma is masked by
a liberal application of various talcum powders, with
Yardley's Lavender always a favourite, and currently it is
this genteel fragrance that dominates, the second subject,
as it were, in her odoriferous concerto.

*Miss Shepherd comes out of the lavatory, pulls down her skirt, and
leaves through the front door. We see something of the inside of the
house and its contents, still at this date, c.1976, fairly uncluttered.*

But as she goes the original theme returns, her own
primary odour now triumphantly restated and left hanging
in the house long after she has departed.

*Out of the window we see Miss Shepherd's van parked in the drive and
Miss Shepherd herself rearranging some plastic bags beneath the van.
She is tall and though her changes of costume will not be described in
detail, she is generally dressed in an assortment of coats and headscarves
but with a variety of other hats superimposed on the headscarves. Old
raincoats figure, as do carpet slippers and skirts which have often been*

lengthened by the simple process of sewing on additional strips of
material. She is about sixty-five.

ALAN BENNETT
(*at the desk, speaks*)

Tell her.

As he watches through the window, A.B. – his other self – comes out
of the house.

EXT. 23 GLOUCESTER CRESCENT. DAY

A.B. approaches the van.

A.B.
(*at the van*)

Miss Shepherd. In future I would prefer it if you didn't use
my lavatory. There are lavatories at the bottom of the High
Street. Use those.

MISS SHEPHERD

They smell. I'm by nature a very clean person. I have a
testimonial for a Clean Room, awarded me some years
ago, and do you know my aunt, herself spotless, said I was
the cleanest of my mother's children –

A.B. gives up, and goes.

– particularly in the unseen places.

INT. 23 GLOUCESTER CRESCENT. STUDY. DAY

A.B. catches Alan Bennett's eye as he passes the study door.

ALAN BENNETT
(*voice-over*)
The writer is double. There is the self who does the
writing and there is the self who does the living. And they
talk. They argue. Writing is talking to one's self, and I've
been doing it all my life, and long before I first saw this
house five years ago.

Cut to:

EXT. 23 GLOUCESTER CRESCENT. DAY

*Five years earlier, possibly with a subtitle, though the unkempt nature
of the house and a 'For Sale' sign indicates that this is earlier. House
empty. No van.*

*A.B. comes round the corner of Inverness Street into Gloucester
Crescent, and then into the garden with an Estate Agent.*

A.B.
Fifteen?

ESTATE AGENT
Number 10 fetched seventeen.

A.B. looks discouraged.

Come on. I thought you had a play on in the West End.
These houses have got so much potential. Once you
get rid of the junk. Well, there you have it: Gloucester
Crescent. Good street. On the up and up.

*A.B. and the Estate Agent walk up Gloucester Crescent. The street is
alive with refurbishing activity. As he speaks workmen bring out a nice*

marble fireplace from No. 63 and shove it in the skip, breaking it in the process. More workmen carry materials into another house.

ESTATE AGENT
Big motor, have you? Loads of room.

INT./EXT. 23 GLOUCESTER CRESCENT. STUDY. DAY

A.B. carries boxes of books into the empty study. Through the window we see two men unloading a table or desk from a removal van. The sign now says 'Sold'.

EXT. 23 GLOUCESTER CRESCENT. DAY

A.B. leaves the house.

EXT. CONVENT. DAY

The van stalled nearby, opposite a convent. From Miss Shepherd's point of view we see A.B., with a W H Smith bag, through the van windscreen which is grimy, with the dashboard hosting a variety of objects like a half-eaten tin of baked beans, a packet of biscuit also half eaten, various tissues, packets of soap flakes etc.

A.B. stops to look at a cross (with a painted crucified Christ). Miss Shepherd appears at his shoulder.

MISS SHEPHERD
You're not St John, are you?

A.B.
St John who?

MISS SHEPHERD

St John. The disciple whom Jesus loved.

A.B.

No. My name's Bennett.

MISS SHEPHERD

Well, if you're not St John I need a push for the van. It's
conked out, the battery possibly. I put some water in only
it hasn't done the trick.

A.B.

Was it distilled water?

MISS SHEPHERD

It was holy water so it doesn't matter if it was distilled or
not. The oil is another possibility.

A.B.

That's not holy too?

MISS SHEPHERD

Holy oil in a van? It would be far too expensive. I want
pushing round the corner.

EXT. CONVENT. DAY

*A.B. starts to push. Miss Shepherd goes though her repertory of hand
signals: 'I am moving off . . . I am turning left' . . . the movements
done with boneless grace and in textbook Highway Code fashion.*

A.B.

Are you wanting to go far?

MISS SHEPHERD

Possibly. I'm in two minds.

EXT. GLOUCESTER CRESCENT. DAY

A police car passes. Miss Shepherd stops the van and crouches down. Miss Shepherd emerges cautiously.

> A.B.
>
> Is that it?

> MISS SHEPHERD
>
> I need the other end.

> A.B.
>
> That's half a mile away.

> MISS SHEPHERD
>
> I'm in dire need of assistance. I'm a sick woman, dying possibly, just looking for a last resting place, somewhere to lay my head. Do you know of anywhere?

A.B. goes.

> ALAN BENNETT
> (*voice-over*)
>
> Bye-bye madam. Mind how you go.

INT. 23 GLOUCESTER CRESCENT. STUDY. DAY

A.B. is back in the study, empty except for the desk and boxes of books piled high, which he has started to unpack.

> ALAN BENNETT
> (*voice-over*)
>
> A proper writer might welcome such an encounter as constituting experience. Me, I have to wait and mull it over.

She saw you coming.

A.B.

She's old.

ALAN BENNETT

You wouldn't get Harold Pinter pushing a van down the street.

A.B.

No. Unlike me. But then, I'm too busy not writing plays, and leading my mad, vigorous creative life.

ALAN BENNETT

Yeah. You live it. I write it.

EXT. GLOUCESTER CRESCENT. DAY

Miss Shepherd's point of view inside the van driving slowly round the street, sussing it out.

As she passes No. 23 her point of view: A.B. outside with his bike, with Rufus and Pauline, neighbours living opposite.

RUFUS

Pretty house, not as big as ours, of course; but you're unattached.

A.B.

No. It's attached to the house behind.

RUFUS

No, you. You're . . . single. Sickert once lived in the street, apparently; Dickens' abandoned wife. Now it's the usual

north London medley: advertising, journalism, TV, people
like you – writers, 'artists'. Anything in the pipeline?

                         A.B.
Well, I've got a play on in the West End.

                        RUFUS
Of course you have. Dare one ask?

                         A.B.
Thirteen five.

                        RUFUS
Oh my God!

                         A.B.
I know.

                       PAULINE
And we're twice as big, so what does that make ours
worth?

                        RUFUS
Mind you, our new neighbour won't help the prices.

Shot of the van now parked at the top of the street.

                         A.B.
Yes, we've met.

                        RUFUS
Last year it was Gloucester Avenue. Now it's our turn.

                       PAULINE
She seems to have settled at 66.

A.B.

Will they mind?

PAULINE

I hope not. We like to think we're a community.

A.B. rides off on his bike.

What play has he got on?

RUFUS

We saw it. That domestic thing.

PAULINE

(*thinks, then shakes her head*)

Gone.

EXT. 42 GLOUCESTER CRESCENT. DAY

Later. Plastic bags being hurled under the van by Miss Shepherd.
Through the open window of No. 42 we hear the sound of children
playing 'London's Burning' on their recorders. As this scene goes on,
another small child arrives, lugging his cello home. Fiona Perry comes
out of the house.

FIONA

(*to Miss Shepherd*)

We thought you might like some pears. They're from our
garden in Suffolk.

MISS SHEPHERD

Pears repeat on me.

She goes on hurling bags.

Were you planning on staying long?

MISS SHEPHERD

Not with that din going on.

Miss Shepherd gets in the van, and closes the door. Fiona goes back into her garden where her husband is waiting.

FIONA

I know what you're thinking. Still, it's nice to feel we're doing our bit for the homeless.

Giles Perry, her husband, says nothing.

INT. 23 GLOUCESTER CRESCENT. STAIRS AND BEDROOM. DAY

A.B. showing a young Actor round. The house is nearly empty.

A.B.

I'd like to keep it like this. Simple.

ACTOR

Monastic.

A.B.

Quite. (*Moving into the bedroom.*) This is my bedroom.

ACTOR

Nice.

A.B.

So do you like being in the play?

ACTOR

Love it. Love it. So English. Just what people want. Bed looks comfortable..

A.B.

Well, maybe you could come round and give me a hand with the decorating.

ACTOR

Sure. My girlfriend's a dab hand at the painting.

The Actor looks out of the window and sees Miss Shepherd pushing her wheelie past.

On hello, darling. You look a character.

A.B.

Well yes, this is Camden Town.

During the course of the film the house should gradually fill up with stuff so that at the finish there's as much clutter (of a superior kind) as the van.

Cut to:

EXT. CAMDEN HIGH STREET. DAY

A.B. gives sixpence to Miss Shepherd, who is sitting on the pavement, which is covered with messages she has chalked up like 'St Francis hurled money from him' and 'Say No to the Common Market'.

There is also a pile of pamphlets, one of which A.B. takes. She is just chalking in some rudimentary birds.

MISS SHEPHERD

Yes, I'm here most days, I teach . . . and the pavement is my blackboard. I also sell pencils. A gentleman came by the other day and said that the pencil he had bought from me was the best pencil on the market at the present time.

A.B.

(*reading leaflet*)

You're against the Common Market, I see.

MISS SHEPHERD

Me? Who said it was me?

A.B.

You're not the writer?

MISS SHEPHERD

Not necessarily. I'll go so far as to say this. They are
anonymous. And they are a shilling. You've only given me
sixpence.

A.B.

(*pointing to the pavement*)

It says there St Francis hurled money from him.

MISS SHEPHERD

Yes, only he was a saint. He could afford to.

PASSER-BY

(*coming out of the bank and tripping over her*)

Sodding beggars.

MISS SHEPHERD

I am not a beggar. I am self-employed. And this gentleman
is my neighbour.

EXT. 42 GLOUCESTER CRESCENT. DAY

Miss Shepherd is putting her bags back in the van.

FIONA

Oh. On the move again? You didn't stay long.

MISS SHEPHERD

No. Because it was non-stop music.

FIONA

Lucy is doing her O-levels.

MISS SHEPHERD

It's the noise levels I'm worried about.

She prepares to move off.

EXT. GLOUCESTER CRESCENT. DAY

Rufus and Pauline in evening dress, with a picnic hamper and blankets, about to get into a cab. They wave to A.B.

RUFUS

Sorry about all this. Glyndebourne.

PAULINE

Cosi.

A.B.

Lucky you. Have fun.

As the cab goes up the street we see Miss Shepherd in her van, doing her elaborate hand signals and slowly moving down the Crescent.

RUFUS

Oh, look out. Madam's on the move.

PAULINE

So whose turn will it be now? (*To the cab driver.*) Slow down.

RUFUS
(*looking at his watch*)
We don't want to miss the curtain.

PAULINE
Mrs Vaughan Williams?

RUFUS
No. The Birts?

PAULINE
Sixty-two?

Elaborate signing from Miss Shepherd that she is coming to a halt.

No. No. No. Darling, that's us.

RUFUS
Stop the cab.

He runs back down the street.

Sorry! You can't park here.

MISS SHEPHERD
I've had guidance this is where it should go.

RUFUS
Guidance? Who from?

MISS SHEPHERD
The Virgin Mary. I spoke to her yesterday. She was outside the post office in Parkway.

RUFUS
What does she know about parking?

PAULINE
(*also having emerged from the cab*)
Rufus! Tell her, we're going to Glyndebourne.

MISS SHEPHERD
I need a ruler. I must measure the distance between the
tyres and the kerb. One and a half inches is the ideal gap.
I came across that in a Catholic motoring magazine under
tips on Christian parking.

RUFUS
This isn't Christian parking. It's a fucking liberty.

They head back up towards the cab.

*They get back into the cab and drive off, some of this encounter having
been seen by A.B.*

EXT. 23 GLOUCESTER CRESCENT. DAY

A.B. calls over to the van, now directly opposite his house.

A.B.
You didn't stay long outside 66.

Miss Shepherd comes over the road to A.B., worried.

MISS SHEPHERD
Not with all that din. They're not musical, are they?

A.B.
Who?

MISS SHEPHERD
Sixty-one.

[112]

A.B.

No. Though they go to the opera. Are you all right?

MISS SHEPHERD

What with all this to-do, I think I'm about to be taken
short. Can I use your lavatory?

She is already on her way into the house.

A.B.

No. The flush is on the blink.

MISS SHEPHERD

I don't mind.

She is in the house. We hear her calling 'Where is it? Where is it?'
before the door bangs and we see A.B.'s agonised face.

INT. 23 GLOUCESTER CRESCENT. DAY

Later. The toilet flushes and Miss Shepherd comes out past him saying
nothing. Furious, A.B. calls after her.

A.B.

'Thank you'?

She ignores him.

INT. 23 GLOUCESTER CRESCENT — LAVATORY. DAY

A.B. scrubs out the lavatory.

EXT. YORKSHIRE COTTAGE. DUSK

A.B.'s mother's cottage, in a village in the Yorkshire dales. Lights are on downstairs. We can see A.B.'s Mam through the window, on the phone.

                              A.B.
                    (*voice-over, on telephone*)
          I've got a meeting at the BBC.

                              MAM
     What about?

                              A.B.
                       (*voice-over*)
          It's just something I'm writing.

                              MAM
     I thought you were coming up.

                              A.B.
                       (*voice-over*)
     In a week or two.

INT. 23 GLOUCESTER CRESCENT/INT. YORKSHIRE COTTAGE. DUSK

A.B. on the phone to his mother. Alan Bennett at the desk.

                              MAM
          I'm on my own.

                              A.B.
          I know you're on your own.

                        ALAN BENNETT
     We're all on our own.

MAM

Can I come down there for a bit? Is it a big house?

A.B.

Not really. You wouldn't like it. Too many stairs.

MAM

They have these chair lift things now. (*Pause.*) Are you still there?

A.B.

Yes.

MAM

The foot feller came today.

A.B.

Who?

Alan Bennett begins to write this exchange down, sat at his writing desk.

MAM

The foot feller.

A.B.

Do you mean the chiropodist?

MAM

You've written that down.

ALAN BENNETT

I haven't.

He has.

MAM

I've given you some script. I'm just raw material.

A.B.

No, you' re not.

Pause.

Mam.

EXT. GLOUCESTER CRESCENT. DAY

Mrs Vaughan Williams rides her bike down the Crescent. Miss Shepherd has her door open, having just got up. She is fanning herself with a fan she has picked up somewhere.

MRS VAUGHAN WILLIAMS

Are you all right?

MISS SHEPHERD

Yes. It's the van. Gets very close.

MRS VAUGHAN WILLIAMS

I imagine.

MISS SHEPHERD

You're tall.

MRS VAUGHAN WILLIAMS

My husband was tall. I'm Mrs Vaughan Williams. I won't shake hands. Gardening.

MISS SHEPHERD

The composer? 'Greensleeves'?

MRS VAUGHAN WILLIAMS

Among other things. Why? Are you musical? I don't even
know your name.

MISS SHEPHERD

It's Miss Shepherd, but I wouldn't want it bandied about.
I'm in an incognito position, possibly.

MRS VAUGHAN WILLIAMS

Safe with me.

EXT. 23 GLOUCESTER CRESCENT. DAY

*Later. Mrs Vaughan Williams talking to A.B. Miss Shepherd in the
background, sorting the plastic bags under the van.*

MRS VAUGHAN WILLIAMS

Shepherd. Drove ambulances in the war, apparently.

A.B.

So where did she spring from?

MRS VAUGHAN WILLIAMS

And a nun once.

A.B.

A nun?

MRS VAUGHAN WILLIAMS

In the convent up the street. Still, everybody's got
something to hide. My brother-in-law's a policeman. That's
Camden. People wash up here. Like me. She'd be a good
subject.

                                A.B.

What for?

                      MRS VAUGHAN WILLIAMS

You. One of your little plays. (*She goes off saying:*)
Remember! I planted the seed!

INT. GLOUCESTER CRESCENT. STUDY. DAY

Alan Bennett is at the desk, his notebook open in front of him.

                          ALAN BENNETT

No, no. I'm writing about Mam half the time as it is. One
old lady's enough.

                                A.B.

I live. You write. That's how it works.

                          ALAN BENNETT

Except you don't much.

                                A.B.

Don't what?

                          ALAN BENNETT

Live. 'Put yourself into what you write.' How? We're both
so fucking tame.

EXT. GLOUCESTER CRESCENT. DAY

*Miss Shepherd is clambering into the van when Lois approaches. In the
van, a battered portable radio is tuned to Radio 4.*

LOIS

Miss Shepherd. I'm Lois, the social worker.

MISS SHEPHERD

I don't want the social worker. I'm about to listen to the repeat of *Any Answers*.

LOIS

I've brought you some clothes. You wrote asking for a coat.

MISS SHEPHERD

Not during *Any Answers*. I'm a busy woman. I only asked for one coat.

LOIS

I brought three, in case you fancied a change.

MISS SHEPHERD

Where am I supposed to put three coats? Besides, green isn't my colour.

She throws the green coat out of the van onto the ground.

Have you got a stick?

LOIS

The council have that in hand. It's been precepted for.

MISS SHEPHERD

Will it be long enough?

LOIS

Yes. It's one of our special sticks.

MISS SHEPHERD

I don't want a special stick. I want an ordinary stick. Only longer. Shut the door.

[119]

LOIS

If I should want to get in touch with you whom should I call?

Miss Shepherd is closing the van doors.

MISS SHEPHERD

You can try Mr Bennett at 23, only don't take any notice of what he says. He's a communist, possibly.

Cut to:

EXT. 23 GLOUCESTER CRESCENT. DAY

A.B. on doorstep of 23 Gloucester Crescent.

A.B.

Have you tried the people opposite, they're nearer?

LOIS

They said they don't relate to her. You were the one she related to.

A.B.

Is that what they said, 'related to'?

LOIS

No. That's me. They said you were her pal. She was your girlfriend.

A.B.

Jesus.

LOIS

Does she use your lavatory?

                    A.B.

Only in an emergency.

                    LOIS

That might give her squatter's rights. We'd be much
happier if she moved on.

                    A.B.

We?

                    LOIS

Camden.

EXT. CAMDEN HIGH STREET. DAY

*Later. Miss Shepherd watches TV though Curry's window: Edward
Heath arriving in Downing Street, 1970.*

A.B. arrives with her shopping.

                    A.B.

I've got everything – sherbet lemons, Cup-a-Soup, the
miniature whisky.

                MISS SHEPHERD

That's medicinal.

*They walk together up the High Street, Miss Shepherd pushing her
child's pushchair.*

                    A.B.

She seemed very understanding, the social worker.

                MISS SHEPHERD

Not understanding enough. I ask for a wheelchair and
what does she get me? A walking stick. (*And she looks*

                    [121]

at him meaningfully.) And she says I don't get an allowance unless I get an address.

A.B.

'The Van, Gloucester Crescent' – isn't that an address?

MISS SHEPHERD

No, it needs to be a house. A residence. Still, I may be going away soon, possibly.

A.B.

How long for?

MISS SHEPHERD

Broadstairs, possibly.

A.B.

Why Broadstairs? Have you family there?

MISS SHEPHERD

No. NO.

A.B.

Have you got any family?

MISS SHEPHERD

I just need the air.

Cut to:

EXT. INVERNESS STREET MARKET. DAY

MISS SHEPHERD

I saw a snake this afternoon. It was coming up Parkway.
It was a long grey snake. It was a boa constrictor, possibly.

A.B.

No . . .

MISS SHEPHERD

It looked poisonous. It was keeping close to the wall. I
have a feeling it may have been heading for the van.

A.B.

No, Miss Shepherd . . .

MISS SHEPHERD

I thought I'd better warn you just to be on the safe side.
I've had some close shaves with snakes.

A.B.

Listen to me, Miss Shepherd. There are no boa constrictors
in Camden Town.

MISS SHEPHERD

Are you calling me a liar? I know a boa constrictor when
I see one.

Pitying smile from A.B. A street trader calls over.

STREET TRADER

All right, my love? You're looking especially lovely today,
sweetheart.

MISS SHEPHERD

Don't sweetheart me. I'm a sick woman. Dying possibly.

STREET TRADER

Well, chin up, love, we all got to go some time. Smells like
you already have.

ALAN BENNETT
(*voice-over*)

I do not believe in the snake, still less that it was en route
for the van.

Cut to:

EXT. 42 GLOUCESTER CRESCENT. DAY

*The Perry children playing in their garden. Piercing scream. Fiona
comes up.*

CHILD (SAM)
Mummy! Mummy! There's a snake!

ALAN BENNETT
(*voice-over*)

Only next day I find there has been a break-in at the local
pet shop, so there may have been a snake on the run ...

A boa constrictor slithers through the flower bed.

So of course I feel guilty.

The children and Fiona run into the house shouting 'A snake! A snake!'

Cut to:

INT. 23 GLOUCESTER CRESCENT. DAY

Alan Bennett sits at his desk, writing.

ALAN BENNETT
(*voice-over*)

A real writer would have asked her about her close shaves
with snakes. Only she seems to have cleared off.

EXT. BROADSTAIRS ESPLANADE. DAY

A bus pulls in. Miss Shepherd gets out.

EXT. BROADSTAIRS STREET. DAY

A Policeman has stopped Miss Shepherd, who is in her usual long skirt etc.

> MISS SHEPHERD
> A nightie? This isn't a nightdress. This style can't have got to Broadstairs yet. And I know the law. You can't be arrested for wearing a nightie.

> POLICEMAN
> What're you doing in Broadstairs?

> MISS SHEPHERD
> I am minding my own business!

EXT. BROADSTAIRS RESIDENTIAL ROAD. DAY

Miss Shepherd is on her way up the hill.

EXT. BROADSTAIRS HOUSING ESTATE. DAY

A suburban housing estate of modest bungalows, backing onto fields.

Miss Shepherd approaches the end bungalow warily. She rings the bell. A solid, respectable man (Mr Fairchild) opens the door. He looks anxiously over his shoulder, shuts the door behind him, and takes Miss Shepherd down the side of the house towards the garden shed.

EXT. YORKSHIRE COTTAGE. DAY

Mam is at the back door.

MAM

Alan! Come out here.

A.B.
(*inside*)

What for?

MAM

There's some massive birds on the wall.

A.B.

There never are. There's nothing on the wall. You're
imagining things.

MAM

There are.

A.B. comes to the door. There are four peacocks on the garden wall.

ALAN BENNETT
(*voice-over*)

And there were, lined up on the garden wall, four peacocks
from the Hall. So, boa constrictors in the street, peacocks
on the wall, it seems that both at the northern and
southern gates of my life stands a deluded woman.

INT. 23 GLOUCESTER CRESCENT, STUDY. DAY

A.B. is back from Yorkshire. Alan Bennett is at the desk.

A.B.

Except you just said they aren't.

ALAN BENNETT

Aren't what?

A.B.

Deluded.

ALAN BENNETT

Well, not in this particular instance.

A.B.

And they're not the same, Alan – Mam and Miss Shepherd.

ALAN BENNETT

No, Alan, they are not. But they are both old ladies.
That appears to be my niche, apparently. And whereas
my contemporaries lovingly chronicle their first tentative
investigations of the opposite sex, or their adventures in
the world of journalism, I'm stuck with old ladies.

He throws his notebook at A.B.

All right – I am keeping a sodding notebook, but only
on the off-chance. She's not a project. She's not in the
pipeline. I don't want to write about her. She's just
something that's happening.

A.B.

So what do you want to write about?

ALAN BENNETT

I want to write about spies.

A.B.

Spies?

ALAN BENNETT

There you are, you see. You think that's barmy. Spies.
Russia. I can't always be writing about the North.
(*Mimicking himself.*) 'I was born and brought up in Leeds
where my father was a butcher, and as a boy I would often
go out on the bike with the orders.' It's not Proust. It's not
even J. B. Priestley.

INT./EXT. 23 GLOUCESTER CRESCENT. BATHROOM. DAY

*A.B. in bathroom brushing his teeth watches: Pauline taking delivery
of a carpet or other upmarket item.*

ALAN BENNETT
(*voice-over*)
The houses in the crescent were built as villas for the
Victorian middle class and their basements are now being
enlarged by couples who are liberal in outlook but not
easy with their new-found prosperity.

*Meanwhile Rufus, leaving home for work with his briefcase etc., passes
Miss Shepherd who is struggling to unscrew a bottle top.*

ALAN BENNETT
(*voice-over*)
Guilt, in a word, which means that in varying degrees they
tolerate Miss Shepherd, their consciences absolved by her
presence.

*Rufus stops and with an ill grace turns back and puts his hand out for
the bottle. He unscrews it and hands it back. All done slightly furtively
lest anyone observe his good turn.*

[128]

EXT. GLOUCESTER CRESCENT. DAY

Snow. The two youngest Perry children come with Fiona and a reluctant Giles and knock on the van door. They have Christmas presents for Miss Shepherd.

PERRY FAMILY

Merry Christmas!

She takes the presents.

MISS SHEPHERD

Shut the door. Shut the door! I'm a busy woman.

They close the van door.

EXT. GLOUCESTER CRESCENT. DAY

Pauline approaches the van with a plate of leftovers, mouthing 'crème brûlée'.

Miss Shepherd takes it gracelessly.

Cut to:

INT. 23 GLOUCESTER CRESCENT. KITCHEN. DAY

A.B. and an Interviewer (American) sit at the kitchen table with a tape recorder.

INTERVIEWER

What was your first play about?

A.B.

Public school – which, more accurately, is what you Americans call private school.

[129]

                    INTERVIEWER
But you didn't go to public school.

                        A.B.
No, but I read about it.

                    INTERVIEWER
And what was your next play about?

                        A.B.
Sex. I read about that too.

EXT. 42 GLOUCESTER CRESCENT. DAY

The Perry children are giving a concert on the pavement, a cap for contributions. Miss Shepherd strides up the street.

                 MISS SHEPHERD
Stop it! Stop it! Stop it this minute! Stop it!

The children flee. Giles comes out of the house.

                      GILES
Do you have a problem?

                 MISS SHEPHERD
They were making a noise.

                      GILES
They're children.

                 MISS SHEPHERD
I am a sick woman.

                      GILES
You certainly are.

                    [130]

A car beeps its horn to get Miss Shepherd out of the road.

EXT./INT. 23 GLOUCESTER CRESCENT. DAY

Miss Shepherd ringing the bell. A.B. opens the door.

> MISS SHEPHERD
>
> Mr Bennett. I've worked out a way of getting on the wireless.

> A.B.
>
> What?

> MISS SHEPHERD
>
> I want to do one of those phone-in programmes. It's something someone like you could get put on in a jiffy.

She pushes past him and goes into the study. A.B. gets in front of her and manages to get some paper on the seat before she sits down. (There is a TV in the corner of the study.)

> I could be called the Lady Behind the Curtain. Or a Woman of Britain, you see. You could take a nom-de-plume view of it. I see the curtain as being here, possibly. Some greeny material would do.

> A.B.
>
> I thought this was a phone-in.

> MISS SHEPHERD
>
> Well?

> A.B.
>
> It's the radio. There's no need for a curtain at all.

MISS SHEPHERD

Yes, well, we can iron out these hiccups when the time comes. And if I come in I could catch up with some civilisation.

A.B.

Civilisation, what you mean the television?

MISS SHEPHERD

Wild life. Famines. Sheep dog trials, possibly. I watch it in Curry's window but it's not ideal.

A look between A.B. and Alan Bennett, who is at the desk.

Je crois que vous passez les vacances en France.

A.B.

Yes. Er, oui.

MISS SHEPHERD

J'ai étudié en France il y a trente-cinq ans.

A.B.

Avant la guerre?

MISS SHEPHERD

What guerre?

A.B.

La guerre mondiale numéro deux.

MISS SHEPHERD

Oui. La deuxième guerre mondiale.

A.B.

Qu'est ce que vous étudiez?

MISS SHEPHERD

I was studying incognito à Paris.

A.B.

But what? What were you studying?

MISS SHEPHERD

Music. The pianoforte, possibly. Have you got an old pan scrub? I'm thinking of painting the van. One of those little mop things they use to wash dishes with would do.

She heads off down the corridor.

A.B.

How about a brush?

MISS SHEPHERD

I've got a brush. It's just for the first coat.

ALAN BENNETT
(*voice-over*)

OK, she's been a nun. Only now it turns out she's been a musician besides, and seemingly with fluent French.

Cut to:

EXT. GLOUCESTER CRESCENT. DAY

Later. Miss Shepherd is painting the van.

ALAN BENNETT
(*voice-over*)

She's certainly no painter. Because today, rain notwithstanding, she moves slowly round her mobile home, thoughtfully touching up the rust patches, with crushed mimosa, always a favourite shade.

Fiona passes with a Child.

CHILD

She's using the wrong paint. Cars have special paint.

MISS SHEPHERD
(*viciously*)

Not this one. It's Catholic paint.

The Child is dragged away.

CHILD

And she smells.

FIONA

That's because she's poor. You'd smell if we were poor.

They pass Mrs Vaughan Williams on the corner of Gloucester Crescent. Mrs Vaughan Williams stands next to A.B.

MRS VAUGHAN WILLIAMS
(*looking at the van*)

Oh ...

MISS SHEPHERD

Telling me about paint. I was in the infants' school. I won a prize for painting.

A.B.

But it's all lumps. You've got to mix it.

MISS SHEPHERD

I have mixed it, only I've got some Madeira cake in it.

ALAN BENNETT
(*voice-over*)

Cake or no cake, all Miss Shepherd's vehicles ended up

looking as if they'd been given a coat of badly made custard or plastered with scrambled eggs.

MRS VAUGHAN WILLIAMS

Divine!

ALAN BENNETT
(*voice-over*)

Still, there were few occasions on which one saw her genuinely happy and one of these was when she was putting paint on.

MRS VAUGHAN WILLIAMS

Jackson Pollock himself could not have done it better. Even with a pan scrub.

An altercation across the street. An official is trying to post a removal order on the windscreen.

A.B. looks up the crescent where council workers are painting yellow lines.

A.B.

Yellow lines.

MRS VAUGHAN WILLIAMS

Sorry?

A.B.

Parking restrictions.

MRS VAUGHAN WILLIAMS

Oh what a bore.

A.B.

She'll be illegally parked. She'll have to move on.

Miss Shepherd is crossing the road with a removal order.

INT. 23 GLOUCESTER CRESCENT. KITCHEN. DAY

A.B. studies the form Miss Shepherd has brought over.

> A.B.
>
> It's a removal order.

> MISS SHEPHERD
>
> I know it's a removal order.

> A.B.
>
> It means you'll have to drive on somewhere else.

> MISS SHEPHERD
>
> But I'm disabled. I don't always use a walking stick and
> that pulls the wool over people's eyes. But I am a bona fide
> resident of Camden and I had rheumatic fever as a child.
> And mumps.

> A.B.
>
> I still think you'll have to move on. Go somewhere else.

> MISS SHEPHERD
>
> Well, it won't move. There's not enough juice.

> A.B.
>
> Well, I'll get you some up the road.

> MISS SHEPHERD
>
> I don't like their petrol. It could go, it just needs a bit
> of coaxing. What I'm worried about particularly are the
> wheels. They're under divine protection. If I do get this
> other vehicle I'd like the wheels transferred.

What other vehicle?

They may be miraculous, the tyres. They've only had to be
pumped up once since 1964.

What 'other vehicle'?

They only cost me a fiver.

Miss Shepherd, you said about another vehicle.

A van.

Another van?

A newer model. A titled Catholic lady says she may get me
one as an act of charity. It's Lady Wiggin only she'd prefer
to remain anonymous.

I bet she would. So why don't you park it outside her
house?

EXT. 12 GLOUCESTER CRESCENT. LADY WIGGIN'S HOUSE. DAY

A.B. at Lady Wiggin's front door.

                              LADY WIGGIN
It's out of the question.

                                    A.B.
There's plenty of room.

                              LADY WIGGIN
I have neighbours.

                                    A.B.
So have I.

                              LADY WIGGIN
So should I not buy her another van?

                                    A.B.
                           (*under his breath*)
Please your fucking self.

                              LADY WIGGIN
What?

EXT. 23 GLOUCESTER CRESCENT. DAY

A.B. returning to the house. Miss Shepherd calls him over.

                           MISS SHEPHERD
Mr Bennett . . . The ideal solution would be off-street
parking. You know a driveway, possibly.

                                    A.B.
So what are you going to do?

                           MISS SHEPHERD
Play it by ear.

EXT. 23 GLOUCESTER CRESCENT. NIGHT

A man in his mid sixties (Underwood), tall and sinister, approaches the van.

UNDERWOOD

Lady. (*Tapping lightly on the side of the van.*) Are you there?

The side window is open a little and he slips his fingers inside.

Is this a bad moment? Have you got something for me?

Miss Shepherd (unseen) bangs his fingers with a hammer or a brick.

You bad bitch! You dirty lying bitch!

He gives the van a great bang. A.B. opens the bathroom window and calls across the road.

A.B.

Can I help you?

UNDERWOOD

Good evening to you, sir. Finding myself in the vicinity, I am taking this opportunity to pay my compliments to Margaret.

A.B.

Margaret?

UNDERWOOD

An old friend from way back. I've been out of the game for a while . . . You know how it is.

A.B.

You mean Miss Shepherd.

UNDERWOOD

Shepherd, is it? Very good.

A.B.

She'll be asleep.

UNDERWOOD

Of course. I will bid you goodnight, sir. I will call again
when my schedule permits.

*A.B. goes inside. Underwood lingers, and taps lightly on the van. Two
twenty-pound notes are slid through the window. He taps again. Then
another twenty-pound note.*

UNDERWOOD

Thank you.

INT. VAN. EARLY MORNING

Miss Shepherd being shaken around – a fairly frightening scene.

INT. 23 GLOUCESTER CRESCENT, STUDY. EARLY MORNING

A.B. looks out of the window and sees a commotion outside.

EXT. GLOUCESTER CRESCENT. EARLY MORNING

*A workman's van, with two young men in their twenties, who get either
side of the van and start shaking it and shouting at Miss Shepherd.*

EXT. 23 GLOUCESTER CRESCENT. EARLY MORNING

A.B. comes out as, jeering, the two guys drive off. A.B. approaches the back of the van.

> A.B.

Miss Shepherd.

No answer.

> Miss Shepherd. Are you all right?

> MISS SHEPHERD
> (*from within the van*)
> I think so. What was it about? It wasn't the police, was it?

> A.B.

No. They were louts. But if you choose to live like this it's what you must expect.

> MISS SHEPHERD

I didn't choose. I was chosen.

INT. 23 GLOUCESTER CRESCENT, STUDY. DAY

A.B. is still in his dressing gown.

> A.B.

Well, that settles it.

> ALAN BENNETT

You think?

> A.B.

I can't always be looking out for her. I'm not her keeper. I mean, what happens to work? I think she should either go ... or ...

Or what?

A.B.

Or bring the van into the drive where we can forget about her. Actually, that's why some men marry . . . so they don't have to think any more about their wives.

ALAN BENNETT

That's not bad.

He is writing it down.

A.B.

Yes. Except it's Proust. And it'll only be for a few months until she decides where she's going. It'll be easier. But it's not kindness.

ALAN BENNETT

No.

He reads from one of his notebooks.

'Good nature, or what is often considered as such, is the most selfish of all virtues: it is nine times out of ten mere indolence of disposition.'

A.B.

That's not you?

ALAN BENNETT

Hazlitt. And it's will. Pure will. She's known what she's wanted all along.

Miss Shepherd is in the confessional with someone on the outside waiting his turn.

MISS SHEPHERD

The soul in question did confess, though in guarded terms, in Rome, in Holy Year, though I'm not sure the priest understood English. Do I look like a joyrider?

PRIEST
(*patiently*)

My child. You have already been given absolution for this particular sin. I have given you it myself on several occasions. Have faith. Absolution is not like a bus pass. It does not run out.

We see Miss Shepherd come out of the box as the next person takes her place and recoils.

MAN

Christ.

PRIEST
(*from behind the grille*)

There is air-freshener behind the Virgin.

The man picks up a can of air-freshener.

INT. 23 GLOUCESTER CRESCENT. KITCHEN. NIGHT

A dinner party in progress: the neighbours and Donald, a young actor, discuss A.B., who is currently not in the room.

MRS VAUGHAN WILLIAMS

He's a saint. Ralph was the same. Some people are just
kind.

RUFUS

Kind? This is London, Ursula. Nobody is kind.

GILES

And now the old cow's got a foot in the door. He's a fool.

MRS VAUGHAN WILLIAMS

Who else would do it?

PAULINE

Well, we might . . . It's just the girls . . .

DONALD

I'm just an unemployed actor and I don't know the lady
but can I ask something? What makes her Alan's problem?

A silence.

MRS VAUGHAN WILLIAMS

Darling. She is a human being.

RUFUS

Only just.

FIONA

(*to Donald*)

Changing the subject. When are we going to find Alan a
girl?

Silence. Giles rolls his eyes. Fiona tries again.

Josephine's pregnant again.

DONALD

Oh no! Actually, I'm just trying to think who Josephine is.

FIONA

The hamster.

A.B. returns carrying a fresh bottle of wine.

A.B.

Here we are.

MRS VAUGHAN WILLIAMS

We were just saying how grateful she'll be.

EXT. GLOUCESTER CRESCENT. DAY

At the van.

MISS SHEPHERD

Put the van in your drive? That hadn't occurred to me.
I don't know. It might not be convenient.

A.B.

No. I've thought it over. Believe me, Miss Shepherd. It's all
right. Just till you sort yourself out.

MISS SHEPHERD

Not convenient for you. Convenient for me. You're not
doing me a favour, you know. I have got other fish to fry.
A man on the pavement told me if I went south of the
river I'd be welcomed with open arms.

*A.B. watches her as she goes back to the van and starts to sort through
her clothes.*

ALAN BENNETT
(*voice-over*)

I was about to do her a good turn but, as ever, it was not
without thoughts of strangulation. She would come into
the garden, yes . . . but only as a favour to me.

EXT. 23 GLOUCESTER CRESCENT. DAY

*Miss Shepherd walks round the old van for the last time. On the
broken windscreen she paints a cross. Her belongings have been piled on
the pavement outside No. 23.*

*We see the council truck towing away the now empty van as the new
(though second-hand) van driven by Miss Shepherd with the usual
battery of hand signals comes down the Crescent.*

*Alan Bennett watches from the study window. The neighbours watch
from the street.*

Van being slowly driven into the drive, comes to a stop (almost).

A.B.
Have you put on the handbrake?

MISS SHEPHERD
I am about to do so.

ALAN BENNETT
(*voice-over*)
Whereupon she applies the handbrake with such
determination that, like Excalibur, it can never afterwards
be released.

A.B. coming into the study, and going to the living-room window.
Behind him, a Young Man comes in, pulling on a shirt or T-shirt.
He has a small overnight bag. A.B.'s point of view of the van, Miss
Shepherd inside, praying, her paraffin light on.

>   ALAN BENNETT
>   (*voice-over*)
> Now she is on the premises, I sometimes get a glimpse
> of Miss Shepherd praying and it is seldom a tranquil or a
> meditative process, the fervour of her intercessions rocking
> her to and fro. What is it she's wanting forgiveness for?
> I used to pray myself when I was young. But never like
> this. I'd never done anything. But what has she done?

INT. VAN. NIGHT

Inside the van, Miss Shepherd prays, a reproduction Assumption of the
Virgin among her possessions.

>   MISS SHEPHERD
> O Virgo Fidelis, first leader of all creatures, intercede on
> my behalf. I hunger and thirst for the fulfilment of a just
> era and utterly trust in possible light received.

INT. 23 GLOUCESTER CRESCENT. STUDY. NIGHT

A.B. turns back to the Young Man on the sofa.

>   YOUNG MAN
> Who's the old bat?

[147]

A.B.

Oh, she's . . . a friend.

YOUNG MAN

A *friend*?

A.B.

Someone I know.

YOUNG MAN

Weird.

A.B.

Maybe.

YOUNG MAN

Actually I think I better be off.

A.B.

Yeah? You don't want to stay for coffee or anything?

YOUNG MAN

Nah.

EXT. 23 GLOUCESTER CRESCENT. NIGHT

From Miss Shepherd's point of view we see A.B. saying goodbye to the Young Man leaving. The Young Man waves at the gate.

A.B. is about to go back inside when Miss Shepherd's hand comes through the window of the van.

MISS SHEPHERD

Mr Bennett. That young man. Did he have an earring?

A.B.

He did.

MISS SHEPHERD

You want to be careful.

Cut to:

INT. 23 GLOUCESTER CRESCENT. KITCHEN. DAY

Mam and A.B. having tea, preparing to leave.

MAM

She'll be wanting to move in next.

ALAN BENNETT
(*voice-over*)

Said my mother, who has been in London on a state visit.

MAM

Why didn't you tell me she was in the drive?

A.B.

I forgot.

MAM

I got a whiff of her when I first came. A right nasty bad dishcloth smell. Well, she's in the garden. Next it'll be the house. What will folks think?

A.B.

This is London. Nobody thinks anything.

MAM

It's with her being a nun, not having got off. They get thwarted. An educated woman and living like that. Mind you, you're going down the same road.

                                A.B.
  Me?

                                MAM
  No cloth on the table. No holder for the toilet roll. Given
  time I could have this place spotless.

                                A.B.
  You've got a home. You wouldn't want to live here.

Mam looks at A.B. It is plain she would like to do just that.

INT./EXT. 23 GLOUCESTER CRESCENT, STAIRS/HALL. DAY

They are climbing the stairs to the hall.

                                MAM
  Where does she go to the lav?

                                A.B.
  It's something to do with plastic bags.

                                MAM
  What sort of plastic bags?

                                A.B.
  Stout ones, I hope. You've not met her, do you want to?

                                MAM
  No. With her being educated I wouldn't know what to say.

A.B. opening the door, the van visible in the doorway. A cab waiting.

  Give us a kiss. When will you be coming up next?

                                A.B.
  Soon.

                            [150]

MAM

The thing is, I keep seeing a car in the car park.

A.B.

That's slightly to be expected, isn't it?

MAM

At night. Watching.

A.B.

Are you taking your tablets?

MAM

When I remember.

She looks out at the van, and Miss Shepherd going about her business.

She should be in a home. Where does she go to the lav?

A.B.

I told you.

MAM

Looked after. A place where they'll wash her and make her presentable. I'm surprised they let her roam the streets.

She walks to the back of the van where Miss Shepherd is sitting.

Good morning.

No response from Miss Shepherd.

ALAN BENNETT
(*voice-over*)

It's like a fairy story. A parable, in which the guilty is gulled into devising a sentence for someone innocent only to find it is their own doom they have pronounced. Because

[151]

my mother is much closer to being put in a home than Miss Shepherd.

Mam gets into the taxi.

A.B.

(*to Mam*)

You got your purse?

MAM

Yes . . . I do miss your dad. Give us a kiss. I asked our Gordon when he was a pilot did he go behind the clouds?

A.B.

And did he?

MAM

I can't remember. He's a love, though. I know that.

Cut to:

EXT. 23 GLOUCESTER CRESCENT. DAY

Miss Shepherd paints the new van yellow.

EXT. 23 GLOUCESTER CRESCENT. DAY

Later, she festoons the van with Union Jacks and other Silver Jubilee paraphernalia.

EXT. YORKSHIRE COTTAGE. DAY

Mam arrives at the front door with her shopping, alone.

INT. VAN. DAY

Two Jehovah's Witnesses come up the drive and ring the front-door bell. A.B. comes to the door.

JEHOVAH'S WITNESS
Good afternoon. Does Jesus Christ dwell in this house?

A.B.
No. Try the van.

EXT. CAMDEN HIGH STREET. DAY

Miss Shepherd at Curry's window watching Mrs Thatcher on TV.

EXT. 23 GLOUCESTER CRESCENT. DAY

Miss Shepherd arrives home with an old TV in her pushchair.

Later: A.B. running an electric cable from the house to the van.

EXT. 23 GLOUCESTER CRESCENT. NIGHT

A.B. watches as another young man leaves the house. The young man looks into the van where Miss Shepherd is watching news coverage of the Falklands War. She sees him peering in.

MISS SHEPHERD
(*in the van*)
Clear off, you nosey blighter!

.EXT. GLOUCESTER CRESCENT. DAY

They come round the corner of Inverness Street and reach No. 23. Miss Shepherd goes towards the van.

MISS SHEPHERD

Mr Bennett.

A.B.

Yes?

MISS SHEPHERD

These men. Who come late at night. I know what they are.

A.B.
(*under his breath*)

Jesus.

MISS SHEPHERD

They're communists. Else why would they come at night?

EXT. 23 GLOUCESTER CRESCENT, GARDEN. DUSK

Miss Shepherd in the van watching television.

Underwood comes into the drive and taps on the van.

UNDERWOOD
(*calling, menacingly*)

I like the new vehicle. Not a mark on it. (*Giving the van a great bang.*) Not a bloody scratch. What's your name now, Margaret?

MISS SHEPHERD
(*from van*)

My name's Mary. Go away.

[154]

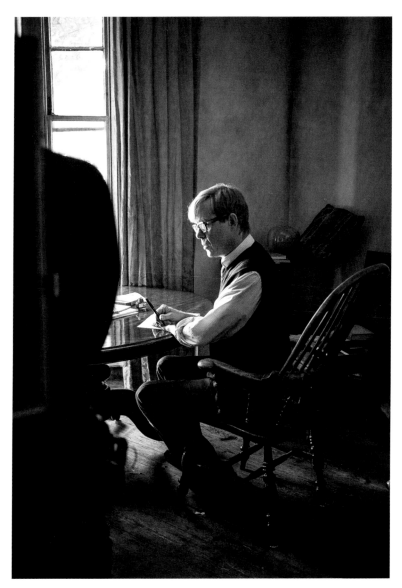

Alex Jennings © *Antony Crolla*

Miss Shepherd's van © *Antony Crolla*

Russell Tovey
Clockwise from foreground: Samuel Barnett, Pandora Colin, Nicholas
Burns, Deborah Findlay, Roger Allam, Frances de la Tour
© *Antony Crolla*

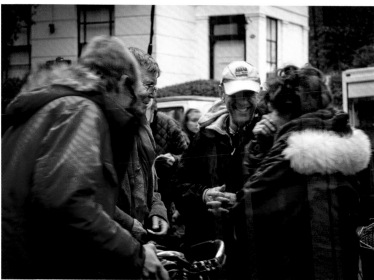

James Corden *Photo: Nicola Dove © Van Productions*
Alex Jennings, Alan Bennett, Nicholas Hytner, Frances de la Tour
  © Antony Crolla

Clockwise from top left: David Gentleman
Alan Bennett and Alex Jennings
Dominic Cooper
Gwen Taylor and Alex Jennings
© *Antony Crolla*

Alex Jennings and Maggie Smith
Clare Hammond and George Fenton
Photos: Nicola Dove © Van Productions

Maggie Smith and George Taylor *Photo: Nicola Dove © Van Productions*
Jim Broadbent
Andrew Dunn and crew
© Antony Crolla

Contents of Miss Shepherd's van
Muffin Green
Rupert Thomas and Alan Bennett
© *Antony Crolla*

UNDERWOOD

Mary is it now? Mary what?

Pause.

Mary what?

He gives a great bang on the side of the van.

MISS SHEPHERD

I'll call the police.

Underwood pulls the van door open. She is cowering inside.

UNDERWOOD

Call the police? I don't think you will, you two-faced pisshole. Because calling the police is just what you didn't do. Apropos of which I think another contribution is due.

Front door opens and A.B. comes out.

A.B.

Can I help you? What's all this din?

UNDERWOOD

No din, sir. Margaret and I were just taking a stroll down memory lane.

MISS SHEPHERD

Don't Margaret me. That name is buried to sin.

A.B.

You came before.

UNDERWOOD

Of course, this isn't *the* van, is it?

A.B.

She had another one.

UNDERWOOD

That is kind of you. A homeless woman. A thankless soul
and not over-salubrious. Goodbye, Margaret.

Beat.

A.B.

I thought you said your name was Mary.

MISS SHEPHERD

It is.

A.B.

Why does he call you Margaret?

MISS SHEPHERD

He's taken too much to drink, on an empty stomach,
possibly.

A.B.

It is your name: Mary Shepherd?

MISS SHEPHERD

Subject to the Roman Catholic Church in her rights and
to amendment, yes.

ALAN BENNETT
(*voice-over*)

It's obviously not her name, and though it's long enough
since she drove the van into the garden, I'm still too polite
to ask who she is; let alone what this fellow wants who
materialises at regular intervals and comes braying on the
side of the van. Music has something to do with it..

Cut to:

INT./EXT. 23 GLOUCESTER CRESCENT, STUDY. NIGHT

Alan Bennett at the desk. Both looking out towards the van. The doors at the back are still open.

> ALAN BENNETT
> (*voice-over*)
> But is it just the noise, or music itself?

A.B. puts some music on.

Through the window they watch Miss Shepherd come out of the van and hurry to the front door.

> MISS SHEPHERD
> (*shouting*)
> I can hear the music. I can hear it. Why must you play that? I can hear it!

A.B goes to the door.

INT./EXT. 23 GLOUCESTER CRESCENT. NIGHT

Miss Shepherd at the door. The music still playing.

> A.B.
> How can you dislike music? You used to play the piano.

> MISS SHEPHERD
> How do you know that?

> A.B.
> You told me.

MISS SHEPHERD

I didn't say I didn't like it. I don't want to hear it, that's all.

A.B. returns to the study.

ALAN BENNETT

Should she speak now? Should she explain?

A.B.

She never lets on. Never explains.

ALAN BENNETT

Well, maybe she should.

MISS SHEPHERD

I was once left alone in a room in the convent.

INT. CONVENT. DAY

We see Young Miss Shepherd, a novice.

MISS SHEPHERD
(*voice-over*)

They didn't leave novices alone normally. And there was
a piano there. I tried it and it was open.

Young Miss Shepherd starts to play. An old nun comes in quietly.

It needed tuning and some of the notes were dead but
it sounded more beautiful to me than any of the pianos
I'd ever played. Then suddenly the mistress of the novices
came in . . . crept in possibly, because I didn't hear her. She
said –

Mistress slams the piano cover.

EXT. 23 GLOUCESTER CRESCENT. NIGHT

> MISS SHEPHERD
> – that was what God wanted. And that I'd been told before. I said – couldn't I just play some hymns for us to sing to? She said that was arguing, and I'd never make a nun if I argued.

EXT. OLD PEOPLE'S HOME. DAY

An Old People's Home overlooking the sea at Weston-super-Mare. A.B. arrives in a taxi.

EXT. OLD PEOPLES HOME. DAY

A.B. sitting beside his mother, on a bench in the garden.

> ALAN BENNETT
> (*voice-over*)
> So with painful symmetry my mother ends up in a home in Weston-super-Mare, while her derelict counterpart now resides in my garden. Putting my mother in a home I see as some sort of failure. And giving the other a home, that's a failure too.

INT./EXT. 23 GLOUCESTER CRESCENT. BATHROOM. DAY

A.B. is upstairs. There is a distant sound getting nearer all the time. Suddenly (and possibly with a bang) we see through the window a three-wheeler Robin Reliant draw up.

> A.B.
> Oh Jesus. She's got herself a three-wheeler.

[159]

EXT. 23 GLOUCESTER CRESCENT. DAY.

A.B. walking round the Reliant, now parked outside the house. Alan Bennett watching from the window.

> A.B.

Where will you park it?

> MISS SHEPHERD

In the residents' parking.

> A.B.

You haven't got a permit.

> MISS SHEPHERD

I have. I got one yesterday.

> A.B.

You never told me.

> MISS SHEPHERD

You'd only have raised objections if I had.

> A.B.

Have you insured it?

> MISS SHEPHERD

I don't need insuring. It's like the van. I'm insured in heaven.

> A.B.

So who pays if you have an accident? The Pope?

> MISS SHEPHERD

I shan't have an accident.

> A.B.

What if you run into something?

MISS SHEPHERD

I shan't run into anything. I'm an experienced driver.
I drove ambulances in the blackout.

A.B.

What if someone runs into you?

Pause.

Miss Shepherd. What if someone runs into you?

MISS SHEPHERD
(*fiercely*)

You have no business saying that.

Pause.

Why do you say that? No one is going to run into me.

Pause.

Where's the key?

A.B.

What key?

MISS SHEPHERD

The car key. I put it down.

A.B.

I haven't got it.

MISS SHEPHERD

You have. You've taken it.

A.B.

I have not.

MISS SHEPHERD

You're lying. You don't want me to have the car so you've taken the key.

A.B.

Don't shout.

MISS SHEPHERD

I have to shout because of your ignorance. People coming and going all hours of the day and night, I'd be better off in a ditch. Give me the key.

A.B.

I haven't got your sodding key. What's that round your neck? This. This.

He pushes her and she falls against the car.

The key. The sodding key.

Mrs Vaughan Williams comes past.

MRS VAUGHAN WILLIAMS

Having fun?

A.B.
(*beat*)

Shouldn't you say sorry?

MISS SHEPHERD

I've no time for sorry. Sorry is for God.

A.B. and Miss Shepherd slowly recover, he watching her retreat into the van. Alan Bennett is at the desk.

ALAN BENNETT
(*voice-over*)
This was the only time I ever touched her. It was not because she was calling me a liar, but because she seemed mad. It was my mother.

A.B.
(*calling through the study window to Alan Bennett*)
It's always Mam you compare her with. They are not the same. I don't like them even sharing the same sentence.

EXT. 23 GLOUCESTER CRESCENT. DAY

A.B. watching at the window.

ALAN BENNETT
(*voice-over*)
These days it's almost as if we're married.

Miss Shepherd is painting the Reliant.

'How's your old lady?' they say. Which is what people call a wife: 'your old lady'.

INT. LYTTELTON THEATRE. NIGHT

A.B. sitting in the stalls during a technical rehearsal with the director of his new play.

DIRECTOR
How's your old lady?

A.B.

She's still there. I'm still here.

DIRECTOR

Your mother died, didn't she?

A.B.

No. She's still here too. She was in hospital, but now she's in a home. Except she's not all there, you know. She's not anywhere.

DIRECTOR

Should we make that plain in the play?

A.B.

No. That's classified information.

Cut to:

EXT. 23 GLOUCESTER CRESCENT. DAY

A.B. watching at the window. Miss Shepherd is painting the Reliant.

ALAN BENNETT

Years ago Mam wanted Miss Shepherd put in a home, but she's still on the loose. Of course, whether she's all there or not is anyone's guess.

She turns towards him and calls through the window. She is splattered with yellow paint.

MISS SHEPHERD

Mr Bennett. I don't like the three-wheeler standing in the street. If you pushed the van in front of your window I could get the Reliant in there on the drive. There's tons of room.

A.B.

So I have the van and the Reliant?

MISS SHEPHERD

I've had guidance that's where it should be. In terms of
vandals.

A.B.

Guidance from whom?

MISS SHEPHERD

I'm not at liberty to speak. I think I may contact my new
social worker.

A.B.

What for? You always say you don't want the social worker.

MISS SHEPHERD
(*returns to painting the Reliant*)
I've had guidance she might help.

INT. 23 GLOUCESTER CRESCENT STUDY. DAY

A.B. now with the new social worker, Miss Briscoe.

A.B.

I don't want a used car lot.

MISS BRISCOE

Mary says . . .

A.B.

Mary who?

MISS BRISCOE

Mary, your Lady in the Van. Didn't you know her name
was Mary?

A.B.

I suppose I did. I always call her Miss Shepherd.

MISS BRISCOE

We all have names. Perhaps if you called her by her name
and she called you by yours? Alan, Mary . . . You never
know, it might be easier to talk things through.

A.B.

Through? There is no through. How do you talk things
through with someone who has conversations with the
Virgin Mary? You talk things through with Isaiah Berlin,
maybe, who in comparison with Miss Shepherd is a man
of few words, but you do not talk things through with her
because you don't get through.

MISS BRISCOE

Alan. I'm getting a bit of hostility here. I realise for you
this may be a steep learning curve . . .

A.B.

No. It is not a steep learning curve. I have never been on
a so-called learning curve. I'm about as likely to be found
on a learning curve as I am on the ski slopes at Zermatt.
And besides, her name isn't Mary.

MISS BRISCOE

Oh?

A.B.

Some people seem to think it's Margaret. And it isn't even Shepherd.

MISS BRISCOE

I have her down as Mary.

A.B.

Yes, and you presumably have her down as a rational human being.

EXT. BROADSTAIRS. DAY

The Reliant pulls up and parks on the front. Miss Shepherd gets out.

EXT. 23 GLOUCESTER CRESCENT. DAY

A.B. comes out with some rubbish. He sees a small brown turd on the side of the bin.

EXT. BROADSTAIRS. DAY

Later: Miss Shepherd on the beach eating chips from newspaper.

EXT. 23 GLOUCESTER CRESCENT. DAY

A.B. has plastic bags over his hands as he begins to remove the turd from the bin.

EXT. BROADSTAIRS. DAY

Then: she sits on a children's carousel, as it revolves carrying her and two or three small children.

INT. BROADSTAIRS ICE CREAM PARLOUR. DAY

Miss Shepherd is served with a large ice-cream sundae.

EXT. CHURCH HALL, ON A ROAD NEAR THE SEAFRONT. DAY

A sign saying SENIOR CITIZENS' CLUB. TEA, COFFEE AND CAKE. ALL WELCOME.

Miss Shepherd goes in.

INT. CHURCH HALL. DAY

A gathering of pensioners. A young woman is about to play the piano.

Miss Shepherd is at the back helping herself to tea and biscuits. She hasn't noticed the pianist. Then the woman plays – Chopin, say. Miss Shepherd is about to flee, hesitates, then stays and listens, transported.

EXT. BROADSTAIRS HOUSING ESTATE. DAY

We see the Reliant Robin slide into view and park not far from the end bungalow, and wait.

A woman (Edith) comes out with a shopping bag. Miss Shepherd crouches down.

INT. GARDEN SHED. DAY

We see Miss Shepherd's slippered feet as she is crammed into a corner.

The door opens. The solid, respectable man comes in, not looking at Miss Shepherd at first.

MR FAIRCHILD
Hello, Margaret.

He looks at her warily.

EXT. ROAD TO BROADSTAIRS. DAY

The Reliant on the road.

EXT. JUNCTION ON COUNTRY ROAD. DAY

Miss Shepherd at the scene of the crash.

She kneels, praying for forgiveness, as a car beeps its horn behind her.

EXT. 23 GLOUCESTER CRESCENT. DAY

The Reliant is back, now parked a little way up the Crescent. A.B. with his bike is trying to look into the van when Rufus and Pauline appear.

RUFUS
What's happened to Stirling Moss? . . . I haven't seen her at the wheel recently.

A.B.
Taking a well-earned break, I imagine. The Dordogne possibly.

[169]

PAULINE

Really?

RUFUS

Pauline.

A.B.

Her car's back. But I haven't seen her around for a bit. I wonder if she's all right.

RUFUS

Am I right in thinking that large many-contoured stain at the back of her frock denotes incontinence?

A.B.

Well, I don't think it's a fashion statement.

PAULINE

Oh, darling. What you must be hoping is that one of these days she'll just slip away.

RUFUS

Don't you believe it. That's what happens in plays. In life going downhill is an uphill job.

PAULINE

How's your mother?

A.B.

Same. Sits. Smiles. Sleeps.

PAULINE

Are you all right?

A.B.

Me? Yes, why? Just going to the theatre.

PAULINE

Not upset about your play?

A.B.

No.

PAULINE

I read a good review the other day.

A.B.

I was told they were all good.

PAULINE

Oh, they are, I'm sure.

RUFUS

We enjoyed it - though I hadn't realised it was just going to be you and nobody else.

A.B.

Well, yes. It's a monologue.

RUFUS

Yes, I suppose. I'm just amazed how you remember it all.

PAULINE

The review I saw was particularly perceptive about you.

A.B.

Really? Saying what?

PAULINE

That you couldn't make your mind up.

A.B.

About what?

> PAULINE

Anything really. It meant in a good way.

> A.B.

Thanks.

A.B. cycles off.

> PAULINE

Actually I couldn't make it out at all. What was it about?

> RUFUS

Him as usual. Not coming clean.

> PAULINE

What about?

> RUFUS

What do you think?

EXT. NATIONAL THEATRE. NIGHT

The National Theatre seen from Waterloo Bridge. On the electronic billboard: 'TALKING HEADS by Alan Bennett'.

INT. LYTTELTON THEATRE. NIGHT

A scene from A Chip in the Sugar.

> A.B.
> *(as Graham)*

'... When I came down again she's still sat there with
her hat and coat on. She said, "Graham. My one aim in
life is for you to be happy. If I thought that by dying it

would make you happy, I would." I said, "Mam, your dying
wouldn't make me happy. In fact the reverse. It would
make me unhappy. Anyway, Mam, you're not going to
die." She said, "No. I'm not going to die. I'm going to get
married. And the honeymoon is in Tenerife. Have one of
your tablets."'

EXT. 23 GLOUCESTER CRESCENT. NIGHT

A.B. cycles down Gloucester Crescent.

> ALAN BENNETT
> (*voice-over*)
> So for the umpteenth time I bike back from the theatre
> where I've been talking about my mother. Though at least
> I know where my mother is.

A.B. taps on the van window.

> A.B.
> Miss Shepherd. Miss Shepherd.

No answer.

> I don't like it.

Alan Bennett has come to the window.

> ALAN BENNETT
> So look in.

> A.B.
> No.

> ALAN BENNETT
> Are you scared?

A.B.

No.

ALAN BENNETT

Not of the body. You're scared this may be the end of the
story and now I'm going to have to write it. Still, now
she's gone I can make it up. Narrative freedom. Whoopee!

A.B.

(*tapping on van*)

Miss Shepherd.

Pause.

Miss Shepherd.

ALAN BENNETT

Go on . . .

A.B. very nervously opens the back door of the van.

Miss Shepherd appears from further up the Crescent.

MISS SHEPHERD

What are you doing?

Both Alan Bennetts react, startled.

Looking at my things?

A.B.

I thought you might be ill. Dead.

MISS SHEPHERD

Dead? Me?

A.B.

I was concerned.

You were nosey.

A.B.

I hadn't seen you. I'm sorry.

A.B. beats a retreat to the house, pursued by Miss Shepherd.

MISS SHEPHERD

I'm not dead. You'll know when I'm dead.

A.B.

I'm sorry.

He goes into the house and shuts the front door.

MISS SHEPHERD

Dead! Me! I shan't die in a hurry, I can tell you. Dead!
Don't make me laugh.

ALAN BENNETT
(*voice-over*)

She didn't die then, and nor did my mother.

Cut to:

INT. OLD PEOPLE'S HOME. DAY

*Through the window, the tide is out. A.B. by Mam's bed, talking to a
Doctor.*

ALAN BENNETT
(*voice-over*)

But as the years passed both of them were beginning to
fade.

[175]

DOCTOR

As you can appreciate it's difficult to take a history but I'm right in thinking she hasn't been a smoker?

A.B.

No.

DOCTOR

Not been a smoker, doesn't drink, all things considered a very healthy woman.

A.B.

You think?

There is an awkward silence.

DOCTOR

This is a woman who has broken her hip. And of course in someone younger and in better circumstances we would give them antibiotics. At your mother's age and in her state of mind, one wonders if this is altogether kind.

A.B.

If you don't give her antibiotics what will happen?

DOCTOR

She may recover or not. She could just sleep away. You mustn't reproach yourself. You've done all . . . more than can be expected.

EXT. 23 GLOUCESTER CRESCENT. DAY

A.B. arrives home by cab. Miss Shepherd is now wheelchair-bound. Her wheelchair has an aerial with a Union Jack pennant.

                           A.B.
                     (*to cab driver*)
Thank you.

                      MISS SHEPHERD
Mr Bennett. Where've you been?

                           A.B.
Seeing my mother.

                      MISS SHEPHERD
How is she?

                           A.B.
The same. She doesn't remember me now.

                      MISS SHEPHERD
I'm not surprised. She doesn't see you very often. Will you
write about me?

Alan Bennett is in the window, writing.

                           A.B.
I don't know. (*Sotto to Alan Bennett.*) She never said this.

                      ALAN BENNETT
So?

                      MISS SHEPHERD
I've heard you on the wireless. Does she know that?

                           A.B.
How can she? She doesn't know who she is.

                      MISS SHEPHERD
That's what you think. Using your mother. You should be
ashamed of yourself.

                          [177]

She didn't say this.

ALAN BENNETT

No, but why shouldn't she?

MISS SHEPHERD

You write about her all the time, one way or another. You
use your mother.

A.B.

That's what writers do.

MISS SHEPHERD

Me next, I suppose. Anyway, now you're here I need some
shopping done.

A.B.

You ought to go yourself. You should try and walk more.

MISS SHEPHERD

I do walk.

A.B.

I never see you.

MISS SHEPHERD

That's because you're not around in the middle of the
night. I want some batteries and some sherbet lemons,
Mr Bennett.

A.B.

Yes.

MISS SHEPHERD

Would you like to push me up the street?

A.B.

Not particularly, no.

EXT. GLOUCESTER CRESCENT. DAY

*But he does and we see him labouring up the street pushing her
wheelchair.*

MISS SHEPHERD
This'll do. Turn me round. Turn me round.

*A.B. turns the wheelchair round. Now at the top of the slope of the
street she pushes herself off with her walking sticks and sails down
the middle of the street, the expression on her face the nearest it's ever
been to pleasure or indeed rapture. It's a real joyride with A.B. rather
alarmed running behind her.*

*When the chair has slowed down, she stops it by slurring her slippered
feet and when it stops she waves her stick in triumph.*

It should be a triumphant scene with lots of music.

A.B.
Are you all right?

MISS SHEPHERD
I think so.

A.B.
Would you like me to make you a cup of coffee?

MISS SHEPHERD
No. I don't want you to go to all that trouble. I'll just have
half a cup.

Later: she gives the coffee cup back to A.B.

I have to go to Mass.

                    A.B.
You're not fit.

          MISS SHEPHERD
It's an anniversary, and a day of obligation.

                    A.B.
Who for? A saint?

          MISS SHEPHERD
No. A young man.

                    A.B.
Someone you loved?

          MISS SHEPHERD
Certainly not. Someone I . . . someone who died. He
would be in his fifties now.

                    A.B.
Was he a Catholic?

          MISS SHEPHERD
Possibly. Only he's in purgatory, he needs my prayers.

                    A.B.
What was his name?

          MISS SHEPHERD
I never bother with names.

*He wheels her off down the Crescent towards Our Lady of Hal, the
RC church.*

INT. OUR LADY OF HAL RC CHURCH. DAY

We see Miss Shepherd at Mass.

When she receives the wafer, she struggles out of the wheelchair and prostrates herself so that the long-suffering priest has to bend right down to get it in her mouth while A.B. (who is there with the wheelchair, waiting to wheel her back) notices the young man serving at Mass.

EXT. CONVENT. DAY

The door of the convent. A woman Housekeeper (not a nun) opens the door.

> HOUSEKEEPER
>
> Yes?

> A.B.
>
> I live down the street.

> HOUSEKEEPER
>
> I've seen you. It's you that has the van.

> A.B.
>
> Yes.

> HOUSEKEEPER
>
> Difficult woman.

> A.B.
>
> A Catholic.

> HOUSEKEEPER
>
> One of the sisters remembers her.

INT. CONVENT. DAY

A.B. and the Housekeeper.

> A.B.
>
> I've been told she was very argumentative. Is that why she was made to leave?

> HOUSEKEEPER
>
> Disputatious she was. I've had her pointed out to me on that account. Hankering after the piano. She always thought she was right but she wasn't right. God is right, end of story. Anyway, what do you want to know for?

> A.B.
>
> She's ill.

> HOUSEKEEPER
>
> Who? The woman?

> A.B.
>
> I wondered if there was a nun available who could talk to her, do her some shopping.

> HOUSEKEEPER
>
> We don't have shopping nuns. It's a strict order.

> A.B.
>
> I've seen them shopping. I saw one yesterday in Marks and Spencer. She was buying meringues.

> HOUSEKEEPER
>
> The Bishop may have been coming.

> A.B.
>
> Does he like meringues?

Who are you, coming round asking if the Bishop likes
meringues? Are you a communist?

A.B.

But she's ill. She's a Catholic. I think she may be dying.

HOUSEKEEPER

They can pray for her, only you'll have to fill in a form.
She'll probably pull her socks up once your back is turned.
That's been my experience where invalids are concerned.

She leaves the room, heading for the exit.

This way out. I don't want you bumping into the sisters.

EXT. 23 GLOUCESTER CRESCENT. DAY

*A.B. is coming in at the gate. There are bits of screwed up paper on the
path. He slips on something. It is plainly shit.*

INT. 23 GLOUCESTER CRESCENT. KITCHEN. DAY

A.B. walks in with his shoe in his hand. Alan Bennett watching.

A.B.

Another parcel on the path.

ALAN BENNETT

If . . . when I write about all this, people will say there's
too much about shit.

A.B. washing his shoe in the sink.

ALAN BENNETT
(*voice-over*)
But there was a lot about shit. Shit was in the forefront.
Caring . . . which is not a word I like . . . caring is about
shit.

INT. 23 GLOUCESTER CRESCENT. STUDY/HALL. DAY

*Through the window we see Miss Shepherd in deep conversation with
Miss Briscoe. Miss Briscoe comes to the front door and rings, A.B.
letting her in, Miss Shepherd watching resentfully.*

MISS BRISCOE
I've talked to Mary.

A.B.
Or Margaret.

MISS BRISCOE
Or Margaret. Miss Shepherd anyway. She tells me you
don't encourage her to get out and lead a more purposeful
life. And put obstacles in her way.

A.B.
I don't encourage her to think she can become Prime
Minister; I do encourage her to try and get to the
supermarket.

MISS BRISCOE
Yes. A carer will often feel that he or she . . .

A.B.
Excuse me. May I stop you? Do not call me the carer. I am
not the carer. I hate caring. I hate the thought. I hate the

[184]

word. I do not care and I do not care for. I am here; she is there. There is no caring.

MISS BRISCOE

Alan, I'm sensing hostility again. (*Pause.*) You see, I am wondering whether, having cared for Mary as it were single-handed for all these years, you don't, understandably, resent it when the professionals lend a hand.

A.B.

No. Though I resent it when the professionals turn up every three months or so and try to tell me what this woman, whom I have coped with on a daily basis for the past fifteen years, is like.

MISS BRISCOE

What is she like?

A.B.

Mary, as you call her, is a bigoted, blinkered, cantankerous, devious, unforgiving, self-serving, rank, rude, car-mad cow. Which is to say nothing of her flying faeces and her ability to extrude from her withered buttocks turds of such force that they land a yard from the back of the van and their presumed point of exit.

Beat. Alan Bennett is at the desk.

ALAN BENNETT

Though of course you didn't say any of that.

Miss Briscoe leaves the study.

People would think that was because you were too nice, it's actually because you're too timid.

Yes. Though this being England, timid is good too.

A.B. goes into the hallway where Miss Briscoe is waiting.

MISS BRISCOE
Well this has been very helpful. I'll see about getting her a doctor.

Cut to:

EXT. 23 GLOUCESTER CRESCENT. DAY

MISS SHEPHERD
(*from inside van*)
Is it a man doctor?

A.B.
Yes.

MISS SHEPHERD
I don't want a man doctor. Don't they have a woman?

DOCTOR
Miss Shepherd, I only want to take your pulse.

MISS SHEPHERD
Which hand? Do you have a preference?

DOCTOR
No.

Miss Shepherd puts her hand through the window.

MISS SHEPHERD
It's normally cleaner than that.

DOCTOR

Miss Shepherd. I'd like to take you into hospital for a day
or so, just to run some tests.

MISS SHEPHERD

I've always had great faith in onions.

DOCTOR

Yes. Onions can only take you so far, medically speaking.

Miss Shepherd closes the van window.

INT. 23 GLOUCESTER CRESCENT/EXT. PHONE BOX. DAY

A.B. and Miss Briscoe are on the phone.

A.B.

She won't go into hospital.

MISS BRISCOE

How do you know?

A.B.

Ask her.

MISS BRISCOE

Would she go to the day centre? She could be looked at
there. And she could stay for a few days

A.B.

She won't go to the day centre.

MISS BRISCOE

Are you sure? Have you asked her?

She will not go to the day centre. I know.

EXT. 23 GLOUCESTER CRESCENT. DAY

MISS SHEPHERD

Of course I'll go. They won't make me stay in?

The back doors of the van are open. Miss Shepherd slides herself out on her bottom as Miss Briscoe confers with an Ambulance Man beside an ambulance parked outside the house.

A.B.

No. They're going to give you a bath and put you in some clean clothes and do some tests.

MISS SHEPHERD

Will they leave me to it?

A.B.

Where?

MISS SHEPHERD

In the bath. I know how to bath myself. I've won awards for that.

A.B.

Yes. I remember.

MISS SHEPHERD

Mr Bennett.

A.B.

Yes?

MISS SHEPHERD

It won't look as if I'm being taken away, will it?

A.B.

Taken away where?

MISS SHEPHERD

Where they take people because they're not right. Do they do that still?

A.B.

Sometimes, but you need a lot of signatures.

MISS SHEPHERD

They pretend things to get you there sometimes. That's the danger with next of kin. It's one of their tricks. They might be pretending it's a day centre.

A.B.

No.

MISS SHEPHERD

I've been had like that once before.

MISS BRISCOE

Alan . . .

The Ambulance Men help Miss Shepherd out of the van.

AMBULANCE MAN

Miss Shepherd.

MISS SHEPHERD

Now I'm a bit behindhand with things so there may be a bit of a d—

AMBULANCE MAN

Put your arm around my neck.

She does.

MISS SHEPHERD

Oh. I've not gone in for this kind of thing much.

The Ambulance Men help her into her wheelchair.

ALAN BENNETT
(*voice-over*)

I note how with none of my own distaste the ambulance driver does not hesitate to touch Miss Shepherd and even puts his arm round her as he lowers her into the chair. I note too his careful rearrangement of her greasy clothing, pulling the skirt down over her knees in the interest of modesty.

MISS SHEPHERD

I'm coming back, you know. This isn't a toe-in-the-water job.

MISS BRISCOE

Is there anything you would like us to take and have us wash?

MISS SHEPHERD

Why? Most of my things are clean.

Neighbours watch, Pauline and Rufus from the steps opposite, as an Ambulance Man wheels her to the ambulance and puts the chair on the lift.

                        PAULINE
                     (*calling across*)
Not ill, your friend.

                         A.B.
No.

                         RUFUS
                       (*hopeful*)
Not going?

              MRS VAUGHAN WILLIAMS
Only to the day centre, apparently.

                         FIONA
                     (*joining them*)
The children always ask after her. They used to be so
frightened of her when they were young. One of them's
in Washington now. The World Bank.

              MRS VAUGHAN WILLIAMS
How long has it been. Ten years?

                         FIONA
More like fifteen.

                         GILES
                      (*together*)
A lifetime.

                    MISS SHEPHERD
Mr Bennett. That social worker wanted to know my next
of kin. I don't want my next of kin broadcast so I said
I didn't have any. Only they're in this envelope.

She gives it him.

Keep it under your hat. (*To the Ambulance Driver.*) I was
an ambulance driver myself once, during the war. I knew
Kensington in the blackout.

> AMBULANCE MAN

Oh really?

The lift rises.

> ALAN BENNETT
> (*voice-over*)

The chair goes up on a lift and in this small ascension
when she slowly rises above the level of the garden wall
there is a vagabond nobility about her, a derelict Nobel
prize-winner she looks, her grimy face set in a kind of
resigned satisfaction.

> MISS SHEPHERD

Could we do that again? I'd like another go.

> AMBULANCE MAN

When you come back.

*Miss Shepherd is wheeled into the ambulance. The Ambulance Men
close the doors. It seems pretty final.*

INT. 23 GLOUCESTER CRESCENT, STUDY. DAY

*A.B. sits looking at the next-of-kin envelope. It is marked: 'Mr.
Bennett, if necessary'. He opens it. On a slip of paper: 'NEXT OF
KIN, LEOPOLD GEORGE FAIRCHILD' and a telephone
number.*

INT. DAY CENTRE BATHROOM. DAY

Miss Shepherd is brought into the bathroom by the Day Centre Worker and confronted with a full bath of steaming hot water.

INT. DAY CENTRE CORRIDOR. DAY

Miss Shepherd, now clean, wearing a dressing gown, is brought down the corridor by the Day Centre Worker.

INT. DAY CENTRE BEDROOM. DAY

Day Centre Worker combs Miss Shepherd's newly clean hair and ties it back.

> DAY CENTRE WORKER
> (*to Miss Shepherd*)

There! Your MOT.

INT. DAY CENTRE RECEPTION AREA. DAY

Lunch is being served at the servery. Seven or eight old people are sitting at tables eating lunch (mince, potato and peas). Miss Shepherd, now in clean clothes, is sitting alone at one table. The Day Centre Worker brings her lunch to her.

A Woman comes and sits at Miss Shepherd's table.

> WOMAN

Hello Margaret.

Miss Shepherd looks at her.

EXT. BROADSTAIRS HOUSING ESTATE. DAY

A.B. arriving at Mr Fairchild's bungalow in a local taxi.

Cut to:

INT. MR FAIRCHILD'S BUNGALOW. DAY

Mr Fairchild, his wife Edith and A.B. having tea.

> MR FAIRCHILD
>
> Fourteen years? You must be a saint. Difficult woman, my
> sister. Edith won't have her in the house.

Edith smiles wanly.

> A.B.
>
> No, I'm not a saint. Just lazy. I know she was an ambulance
> driver.

> MR FAIRCHILD
>
> Yes. And a nun. Twice over, till they got rid of her. She
> spent some time in an an asylum. Banstead. Which was
> my fault.

> EDITH
>
> No.

> MR FAIRCHILD
>
> Mind you, she was a difficult woman. And such a bully.

> A.B.
>
> Did she bully you? She bullies me.

> MR FAIRCHILD
>
> I had her put away. Incarcerated. Sectioned, is what you

call it today. Mind you, she got away from them too. Gave them the slip. Does she still play? The piano.

> A.B.

No.

> MR FAIRCHILD

That is sad. Have you heard of Cortot? Alfred Cortot, the virtuoso pianist.

> A.B.

Yes . . .

He gets up and goes to the cabinet, finds a record.

> MR FAIRCHILD

Margaret was his pupil. She had to go over to Paris for lessons. Wasn't easy in those days. And practised. Oh my word, she used to practise all day long. Only the nuns put a stop to that. I was a vet in Africa and when I came back the music was out. Finished. Practising had become praying.

He drops the needle on the record.

Played at the Proms once.

The record plays. They listen. The music takes us back to —

INT. CONCERT HALL. NIGHT

The 1938 concert from the title sequence, which we see again. The camera moves in on the pianist, and we see that she is the young Miss Shepherd.

INT. DAY CENTRE RECEPTION AREA. NIGHT.

As Miss Shepherd is crossing the reception room, dark except for a single night light, she sees a piano. She stops, drawn to it in spite of herself. She goes to it, opens it. Her arthritic but newly clean hands touch the keyboard. She tentatively plays the first bars of the slow movement, full of mistakes. Stops. Tries again. Stops.

Then, as if the memory is in her muscles, her fingers move across the keys and she plays an an elaborately beautiful passage from the middle of the movement, almost to perfection. The music takes her over.

EXT. 23 GLOUCESTER CRESCENT. NIGHT

The music continues to play.

A.B. walks up the drive, carrying a bunch of flowers, and passes the van. He taps on van door.

A.B.

Miss Shepherd? Miss Shepherd?

He opens the van door.

I just tried to visit you.

MISS SHEPHERD

I wasn't stopping there. A woman said my face rang a bell. Was I ever in Banstead? And would not stop. They gave me some mince. She said, you'll find the mince here a step up from the mince in Banstead. I don't know about the mince in Banstead, or anywhere else for that matter. It's where they put people when they're not right.

A.B.

Well, you look nice and clean.

MISS SHEPHERD

That will be the bath. They let me do it myself, only the
nurse came and gave me some finishing touches. She said
I'd come up a treat.

A.B. offers her the bunch of flowers.

A.B.

I bought you these.

MISS SHEPHERD

Flowers? What do I want with flowers? They only die. I've
got enough on my plate without flowers . . .

A.B.

You won't often have been given flowers.

MISS SHEPHERD

Who says? I've had bigger flowers than these and with
ribbons on. These don't compare. (*Pause.*) Music. How
are people supposed to avoid it? You see I had it at my
fingertips. I had it in my bones. I could play in the dark,
had to sometimes. And the keys were like rooms. C Major.
D Minor. Dark rooms. Light rooms. It was like a mansion
to me, music.

Pause.

Only it worried me that playing came easier than praying.
And I said this, which may have been a error.

Said it to whom?

MISS SHEPHERD

My confessor. He said that was another vent the devil could creep through. So he outlawed the piano. Put paid to music generally. Said that dividends would accrue in terms of growth of the spirit. Which they did. They did.

Pause.

How is your mother?

A.B.

The same.

MISS SHEPHERD

Still in the coma?

A.B.

No.

MISS SHEPHERD

Just getting a bit of shut-eye. People do.

A.B.

Good night.

MISS SHEPHERD

Mr Bennett. Hold my hand. It's clean.

He does. Closes the van door and walks towards the house.

ALAN BENNETT
(*voice-over*)

Some of what this woman had been I found out after she died, so with her life a deliberate mystery . . .

Cut to:

INT. 23 GLOUCESTER CRESCENT. DAY

A.B. at the window.

> ALAN BENNETT
> (*voice-over*)
> To tell it I have occasionally had to invent, though much
> of it one could not make up. And I do not make it up
> when I say that it was on the morning after this talk,
> when she lay in the van with clean clothes and with her
> hair washed, that on that same morning comes the social
> worker into the garden, bearing clean clothes, linen and
> ointment and knocks on the door of the van.

EXT. 23 GLOUCESTER CRESCENT. DAY

Miss Briscoe at the van door.

> MISS BRISCOE
> Mary. (*She knocks on van.*) Mary?

A.B. and Alan Bennett watch from inside. She opens the door.

EXT. 23 GLOUCESTER CRESCENT, DAY

*A.B. arrives at the van door with Miss Briscoe. Miss Shepherd lies
dead inside.*

> ALAN BENNETT
> (*voice-over*)
> It is a van no longer. It is a sepulchre. Even now I do not
> venture into this evil-smelling tomb. I feel cheated that

the discovery of the body has not actually been mine and that, having observed so much for so long, I am not the first to witness her death. Now in quick succession come the doctor, the priest and men from the undertaker's, all of whom this cold winter morning do what no one else has done for twenty years: namely without pause and seemingly without distaste step inside the van.

We see the undertaker's men take out the body in an ordinary-seeming box.

INT. OUR LADY OF HAL RC CHURCH. DAY

The funeral. The coffin is in front of the altar. The Fairchilds in the front pew. The neighbours behind.

> PRIEST
> Lord, grant her everlasting rest and let perpetual light shine upon her. Present her to God the most high.

As the Priest continues, a man materialises behind A.B. It is Underwood, Miss Shepherd's visitor.

> UNDERWOOD
> (*quietly*)
> She's gone then, the lady. (*Indicating the Priest.*) He would know. She'll have told him. Only they got to keep mum, vicars. No helping the police with their enquiries. Did you know she was on the run?

> A.B.
> Miss Shepherd?

Cut to:

EXT. ROAD TO BROADSTAIRS. DAY

Flashback. The junction. The motorbike slams into the van. The Young Biker's face smashes into the windscreen. The Young Biker dead on the road. Miss Shepherd at his side. She gets back into the van and drives off.

> UNDERWOOD
> (*voice-over*)
> Miss whatever you called her. Oh yes. Stationary at a junction a young lad on a motorbike comes round a corner too fast. Smashes into her vehicle.

INT. OUR LADY OF HAL RC CHURCH. DAY

> UNDERWOOD
> Not her fault. Only here's a dead boy on the road, whom she thinks she's killed. Does she call the police? Flag down a fellow motorist? Oh no. She clears off pronto, thereby putting herself on the wrong side of the law.

> A.B.
> So you blackmailed her?

> UNDERWOOD
> I am a policeman, Mr Bennett. Retired of course, but we don't do things like that.

EXT. OUR LADY OF HAL RC CHURCH. DAY

The coffin is slid into the hearse.

RUFUS

Well, it's a cut above her previous vehicle.

ALAN BENNETT
(*voice-over*)

All those years stood on my doorstep she was outside the law. A life – this is what I keep thinking – a life beside which mine is just dull.

EXT. GRAVEYARD. DAY

A.B. is alone at the grave. The undertaker's men hover nearby.

ALAN BENNETT
(*voice-over*)

Left to my own thoughts at the graveside, one of the undertaker's men takes my eye. Not an occupation one drifts into, I imagine . . .

MISS SHEPHERD
(*who materialises behind him*)

Mr Bennett, excuse me, I'm supposed to be the centrepiece here.

ALAN BENNETT
(*voice-over*)

But I'm forgetting that the dead know everything.

MISS SHEPHERD

You should be fighting back the tears, not eyeing up the talent.

A.B. turns startled to Alan Bennett who is beside him.

ALAN BENNETT

Well, it's a thought. She's dead now. I can do what I want
with her.

MISS SHEPHERD

Yes, you can, I'm dead. Feel free. Oh, hello. There are two
of you now. Is that because you're in two minds?

ALAN BENNETT

Yes.

A.B.

No.

*Miss Shepherd walks away from the grave, the other two catching up
with her.*

MISS SHEPHERD

I've been wondering. Would either of you object if the van
were to become a place of pilgrimage?

ALAN BENNETT

No.

A.B.

I'm getting rid of the van. The van is going.

MISS SHEPHERD

Healing could take place and any proceeds could go
towards the nuns.

A.B.

The nuns! What did the nuns ever do for you?

MISS SHEPHERD

Well, not much, but when the donations start rolling in
they'll realise what a catch I would have been. It was the

same with St Bernadette. They didn't realise with her until
it was too late. This way! There's someone I want you to
meet!

Miss Shepherd turns off the path, looking for someone. They follow.

(*To Alan Bennett.*) That's something you could do. This
thing you're trying to write, you could pump it up a bit.
If it were along the lines of *The Song of Bernadette* it would
make you a packet.

Alan Bennett looks unconvinced.

Why do you just let me die? I'd like to go up into heaven.
An ascension, possibly. A transfiguration.

ALAN BENNETT
That's not really my kind of thing.

*She has found who she's been looking for: a beaming Young Biker,
sitting behind a gravestone, smoking.*

MISS SHEPHERD
There you are. This is my new friend. It's the young man
who crashed into the van.

YOUNG BIKER
Hi.

MISS SHEPHERD
I thought it was me that killed him, only it turns out it was
his own fault, so one way and another we've got heaps to
talk about. Well, goodbye.

She laughs.

Mr Bennett . . .

Yes.

MISS SHEPHERD

I came in to your drive for three months and I stayed for fifteen years!

She continues to laugh.

Mr Bennett.

A.B. AND ALAN BENNETT

Yes.

MISS SHEPHERD

Do you know what that is?

A.B. AND ALAN BENNETT

No.

MISS SHEPHERD

It's the last laugh.

She takes the Young Biker's hand. They walk away. A.B. looks at Alan Bennett. Alan Bennett shrugs.

ALAN BENNETT

Well, she wanted an ascension. Let's answer her prayers. Stand by, Miss Mary Teresa Shepherd, late of 23 Gloucester Crescent. Up you go!

They look back towards Miss Shepherd, who ascends to Heaven.

Cut to:

EXT. 23 GLOUCESTER CRESCENT. DAY.

A.B. cleaning out the van.

> ALAN BENNETT
>
> Starting out as someone incidental to my life . . . She remained on the edge of it so long she became not incidental to it at all.

EXT./INT. OLD PEOPLE'S HOME. DAY

This speech over various shots including A.B. sitting with his mother, who lives on, on a bench overlooking the empty bay at Weston-super-Mare; and A.B. sitting by her bedside.

> ALAN BENNETT
> *(voice-over)*
>
> As homebound sons and daughters looking after their parents think of it as just marking time before their lives start –

EXT. 23 GLOUCESTER CRESCENT. DAY

Later, A.B. is clearing the garden of Miss Shepherd's plastic bags. The outline of the truck visible in flecks of yellow paint. Alan Bennett is at the desk in the window.

> ALAN BENNETT
> *(voice-over)*
>
> – so like them I learned there is no such thing as marking time, and that time marks you. In accommodating her and accommodating to her, I find twenty years of my life has gone.

The van is hauled out of the drive by a salvage truck. The truck driver scrawls 'On Tow' in the dirt on the windscreen. A.B. watches it go.

                    ALAN BENNETT
                     (*voice-over*)
This broken-down old woman, her delusions, and the slow abridgement of her life with all its vehicular permutations, these have been given to me to record . . . as others record journeys across Tibet or Patagonia or the thighs of a dozen women.

Cut to:

INT. 23 GLOUCESTER CRESCENT, STUDY. DAY (1990)

A.B. opens a box containing copies of the first LRB paperback edition of The Lady in in the Van.

                       A.B.
You wanted me to make things happen and I never have much. But it doesn't matter, because what I've learned – and maybe she taught me – is that you don't put yourself into what you write. You find yourself there.

                    ALAN BENNETT
I never wanted to write about her. And if there'd been a bit more in your life, I wouldn't have had to.

                       A.B.
Maybe I will now.

The sound of the key in the front door, which bangs shut. A voice calls 'Hi!'

What?

A.B.

Have a bit more in my life. I might even start living.

A.B. looks towards the Man who now comes through the study door and greets him, and who seems quite at home.

Good day?

MAN

Not bad. You?

A.B. shrugs and the Man puts his hand on his shoulder and leaves it there.

He goes towards the kitchen stairs.

You coming down?

A.B.

All right.

A.B. following him, saying to Alan Bennett as he goes,

It's the end of the story, it might make a play. What do you think?

Alan Bennett still at the desk.

MAN
(*going downstairs*)
Now I'm here I think you should stop talking to yourself.

A.B. looks back at the desk, and the chair is empty. A.B. smiles and follows the Man downstairs.

EXT. 23 GLOUCESTER CRESCENT. DAY (AUTUMN 1990/2014)

Wide on Gloucester Crescent, we see the real Alan Bennett cycling down the road.

In the now empty garden, A.B. and the neighbours conduct a small ceremony to mark the unveiling of a blue plaque on the wall.

With them, a film crew gathered outside 23 Gloucester Crescent making the film.

A.B.

Gloucester Crescent has had many notable residents but none odder or more remarkable than Miss Mary Shepherd to whom we dedicate this blue plaque today.

The plaque reads:

Miss M T Shepherd
'The Lady in the Van'
lived here 1974–1989